Trolleybus
Pilot

It is ninety years since the trolleybus first hummed its way through Wolverhampton's streets and half a century since the last conductor issued his last ticket on the last trolleybus to Fordehouses. It seems appropriate that its small, but unusual, contribution to the training of pilots should be made more widely known.

Trolleybus
Pilot

HOW THE HUMBLE TROLLEYBUS
HELPED TRAIN WARTIME PILOTS

Alun John Richards

y Lolfa

First impression: 2016

© Copyright Alun John Richards and Y Lolfa Cyf., 2016

The contents of this book are subject to copyright, and may
not be reproduced by any means, mechanical or electronic,
without the prior, written consent of the publishers.

Cover design: Y Lolfa

ISBN: 978 1 78461 242 9

Published and printed in Wales
on paper from well-maintained forests by
Y Lolfa Cyf., Talybont, Ceredigion SY24 5HE
website www.ylolfa.com
e-mail ylolfa@ylolfa.com
tel 01970 832 304
fax 832 782

Contents

Introduction

DURING THE 1920s many towns and cities in a surge of civic pride, tore up their skid-provoking cycle-trapping tram tracks, scrapped their ageing, rattling and outmoded tramcars, replacing them with sleek, silent electric trolleybuses. Such vehicles could provide levels of comfort, quietness, reliability and speed, far beyond the capabilities of motorbuses at the time. Moreover, where power stations were municipally owned, fuel costs were negligible. Admittedly overhead wires were needed but the existing tram networks could be readily adapted.

By the 1960s, fixed routes were unacceptable in changing city layouts and motorbus technology was 'streets ahead', so the 'Whispering Wheels' had to go. Often the clincher was the nationalisation of the local power station, which meant that the trolleybuses had to pay market rates for their current.

The quietness and freedom from pollution which their 170 trolleybuses brought to the citizens of Wolverhampton is remembered with nostalgia, their contribution to aviation is scarcely remembered and certainly hitherto unrecorded.

As a child I had no knowledge of trolleybuses, but I certainly had powerful aeronautic ambitions.

However, before my aeronautical ambitions could be realised, I had a lot of growing up to do. Even when this had been accomplished there were many obstacles to be overcome and numerous indignities to be suffered before I could take advantage of the instructional facilities offered by the transport system of this particular Midlands municipality.

1

The Icarus Complex

THE SECOND WORLD War lasted almost six years. By accident of age the war was half over before King George deigned to accept my services. In addition, it took his minions almost a further year and a half to train me to do anything useful. Thus, for almost three-quarters of the war I made no contribution to its winning. In fact, since I consumed valuable food, goods and services, I was actually more of an asset to the Axis powers than to my own side.

Even after my loins were girded for battle, as it were, I was rarely in serious peril other than from my own incompetence; besides, not being called upon to die for my country, I was spared the moral dilemma of causing some other man to die for his. I never suffered any serious discomfort. Apart from the odd night spent in a fetid, overcrowded railway compartment or on a railway station bench, I slept between sheets and was seldom more than half a day's train journey from home. I never heard the proverbial 'shot fired in anger', since the only time I was shot at, I didn't hear it; my assailant failed to persist in his attack, so cannot have been particularly angry.

I am acutely aware that my experience was not typical and that more than 70,000 fellow members of the RAF died, many more were physically maimed or mentally scarred, and even more endured danger, discomfort, degradation and separation.

I pay tribute to the unimaginable bravery of those thousands who rightly received decorations, the tens of thousands whose heroism went unrecognised and unrecorded, and the men of Bomber Command, who faced odds of survival that were statistically negligible. I still find it humbling that I was privileged to wear the cloth of heroes. Indeed I am proud to have served with the countless men and women who played humbler roles with devotion and dedication, yet failed to be allotted such a 'cushy number' as I enjoyed.

However, no matter how excellent and honourable the personnel (well, most of them!) it is difficult to take entirely seriously an organisation founded on All Fools Day – allegedly to use up thousands of yards of serge. This fabric had been intended to clad the Tsar's army for its triumphal march through Berlin, but since both the Tsar and his victory ambitions had vanished, these bales lay unwanted (and unpaid for) in a Bradford warehouse. Anyway, whatever the source, they failed to think of a snappy name for the colour, settling for the rather non-committal Blue/Grey. To that can be added the curious ranks. A 'pilot officer' might be a pilot, but equally he might be a navigator; indeed, he might be a pimply pen pusher. Similarly, a 'flying officer' might be an aviator, but he also might be a myopic stores superintendent who only went 'flying' when he was incautious when walking on a slippery surface. Calling the men who definitely did not fly 'airmen' was farcical, but I was lucky to escape the alleged 1918 proposals that included rankings such as 'reeve', 'banneret', and 'ardian', which had been quarried from medieval archives. Much the same can be said about branches and trades. An officer who flew belonged to the General Duties Branch, but a ranker assigned to General Duties may well find himself cleaning the latrines.

After one had actually accepted the 'king's shilling', both the paradoxical and the ridiculous became commonplace, as, for instance, when patrolling an insignificant Midlands airfield. My companion and I were issued with a rifle and instructed to challenge any person acting in a 'suspicious manner'. This challenge involved pointing one's (unloaded) rifle at the suspect and stoutly calling: 'Halt, who goes there?' In stygian darkness, the direction in which the rifle was pointed would of necessity be approximate; come to think of it, how would you know anyone was there in the first place? In any case what could be considered a 'suspicious manner'?

Theoretically, the challengee would reply, 'Friend'.

One was then supposed to say: 'Advance, friend, and be recognised', although how one would recognise even one's best friend without a torch (which blackout regulations barred) was not clear.

Should the person fail to account for himself satisfactorily, and despite being about as far from the sea as it is possible to be within the UK, one had to assume that he had recently vacated a Nazi submarine. The possibility that said dastardly Nazi would answer 'friend', and when invited to advance would stick a knife in you, was never entertained. Again, the problem of language was never addressed, although if he was a properly trained spy presumably his English would be impeccable; but then also, one assumes, would be his credentials.

However, if the said Nazi was stupid enough to answer 'Foe', presumably one of us would try to persuade the intruder to stay where he was, whilst the other of us groped his way to the mile-distant guardroom to appraise the guard NCO of the problem. The latter would then send a runner to rouse the orderly officer, who would then rouse the duty armourer and accompany him to the ammunition store and obtain (against signature of course) the appropriate ammunition. The runner would deliver this to the NCO i/c guard who would issue the rounds, again against signature. The 'guard' would then attempt to re-locate his companion and the intruder, and presumably shoot the latter.

There was a snag in this well-thought-out plan. Our rifles were American P17s (and yes, the '17' did refer to the year of design), which outwardly resembled a British SM Lee-Enfield. The P17s used .300 ammunition but, so rumour had it, only .303 Lee-Enfield rounds were stocked in the armoury.

This, of course, was well down the road, when I had actually commenced my flying training. In the months up to this point I suffered numerous humiliations, every one of which put my sense of humour to the test.

When war broke out in 1939, I had no real grasp of the horrors of war, and so I did not share the grown-ups' dismay. I merely felt annoyance that matters could not have been postponed until I was old enough to take part. This anxiety was, I am ashamed to admit, not due to patriotic fervour, but because of the opportunity the war afforded to fly an aeroplane.

I had been aviationally orientated since I could count my age on my fingers and still have digits to spare. Having flown five times with various 'Air Circuses' I considered myself something of a veteran of the skies. In addition, study of the external control cables on an Avro 504 on Swansea sands had given me a sound knowledge of how to control a flying machine.

The Fleet Air Arm offered great glamour, but I did prefer to return from mortal combat to a runway (and a bed!) that kept still. During the lull before the storm, the 'Phoney War', the RAF was not allowed to drop bombs on Germany. They were only permitted to drop leaflets, and it was said that they had to be careful not to release whole packets in case they hurt some poor Stormtrooper. Inevitably, this caused the Air Force to be unfairly criticized, attracting epithets such as 'Brylcreem boys' and the 'Royal Air Farce'. They did themselves no favours with their poster campaign showing a clean-cut officer pilot scanning the sky. This attracted suggestions that the smile on his face was due to his intention to have his wicked way with the WAAF at his side (and that she was smiling for the same reason). Deluged with these and other posters, it was no wonder that folk talked about the 'Royal Advertising Force'.

The Royal Air Force was then like a gentlemen's club, women being denied full membership. In fact the Women's Auxiliary Air Force invariably did a better job than their male counterparts. In these early months of the war the press fulminated about the 'scandalous immorality' that allegedly occurred when service men and women were 'thrown together'. This was undoubtedly government-inspired, to back up the subliminal inference in the advertisements that there would be certain 'opportunities' for recruits; thus encouraging recruitment. If any men joined up as a result, they must have been sadly disappointed.

Following the Battle of Britain in the summer of 1940 the perception changed. Everyone in a light blue uniform became an instant hero, even if they were only RAC patrolmen, cinema commissionaires or brass bandsmen. After London and other cities were bombed, the RAF were allowed to drop real bombs on Germany, and news of even the puniest air raid on Germany was greeted by cheering in the streets. Thus when the Air Training Corps (ATC) offered youngsters the chance to wear the coverted Air Force blue, there was a stampede. For me, the ATC was something of a disappointment. Having been persuaded to join the school squadron as opposed to a town unit, my schoolfellows and I were denied the leadership of able ex-RAF and RFC officers, and by the time we received our uniforms we had outgrown them. Indeed, the ATC as a whole was bit of a con, as the authorities were putting about the impression that membership would guarantee priority when aircrew were being selected.

Leaving school for university, I found that the University Air Squadron (UAS) was very different from the ATC. We wore proper RAF uniforms complete with the eagle badges ('shoulder shitehawks'), and the official 'Aircrew Under Training' white flash on our caps. The only snag was that our buttons and badges were of chrome rather than brass, like the genuine article. Thus, only the most myopic young woman would mistake us for the real thing, which seriously restricted our chances of being greeted horizontally as heroes. Also, barmaids would spot the ATC accoutrements, so any demand for an alcoholic beverage was liable to be greeted with: 'Hop it, sonny, you're under age'.

We formed an unusual group within the university since we were pledged to join up as soon as possible, while the majority of the student body had the reverse intention. Some dodged about picking courses that carried deferment from call-up. Paradoxically, such deferment carried a requirement to join the college Home Guard. Thus, in contrast with the usual perception of the Home Guard as impatient to 'have a crack at the enemy', this unit took the opposite view.

Despite being in real life lecturers in the English department, the two elderly UAS officers were competent, charismatic, dedicated and knowledgeable, and wore WWI medal ribbons. The flight sergeant instructor was a most able man, an air gunner, who was being 'rested' after being awarded the Distinguished Flying Medal (DFM) for attempting to destroy the bridge at Maastricht in May 1940.

As well as learning a great deal, the UAS brought us into contact with the actual RAF at the local balloon barrage unit, and the air gunnery school at Stormy Down. Not only did we get a ride in an Armstrong Whitley A.W.38 Whitley bomber at Stormy, both barrage unit and gunnery school prepared us for the shock/horror we would suffer when we actually joined up.

My first experience of staying overnight on RAF property was certainly not agreeable. The stay took place at RAF Penarth where, in a collection of houses, shops and halls, one was pummelled, prodded and examined from brains to boots, and pronounced fit. The food was vile, the beds were hard and cold, and almost as soon as one had eventually slept one was roused by a humanoid disguised as a corporal, and beset on all sides by airmen fervently encouraging me to get out while I could. Despite all this, I allowed myself to be sworn in as one of the king's liegemen.

Even more serious was summer camp at RAF Fairwood Common. Most of us had watched from afar the Defiants, Whirlwinds and, later, Beaufighters taking off and landing, and had heard engines being run up and glimpsed vehicles moving about. How different it was in reality... just as from a distance an anthill looks almost lifeless, but if broken open reveals a teeming mass of activity.

Everyone seemed to be hurrying intent on some vital task.

We soon found that only some were actually employed with said vital tasks; everyone else was queuing. They seemed to be queuing for everything, but mostly for food. As soon as breakfast finished the dinner queue would form. None of us had realised how spread out everything was. We were accommodated in the living site nearest to the domestic site (where one queued to eat, queued to wash and queued to use the lavatory), but it was still a 20-minute jog trot away. We were in a tin hut that had a loudspeaker (a very loud speaker), which woke us around dawn. In fact it was good taster of what would in a few weeks befall us all.

Agreed, we met the mighty men who flew the Beaufighters; we played with lots of interesting bits of kit, and were lectured by the commanding officer, Wing Commander 'Batchy'Atcherley (later Air Vice Marshal Sir Richard Atcherley. His identical twin brother David (later also a knight and an AVM) succeeded him as O/C RAF Fairwood Common).

Even so, we were tempted when, as at Penarth, we were advised to desert and join the army – any army, the Salvation Army if need be. We possibly would have followed this advice had it not been for the UAS aeroplane.

It was a De Havilland Moth Minor, now an all-but-forgotten-type intended as a replacement for the Tiger Moth. There was no proper instructor so we had to rely on the goodwill of any spare Beaufighter pilot.

I was strapped in, the engine was started, the pilot taxied onto the runway (22 as we now know it), lined up, and through the speaking tubes came his voice: 'Open the throttle smoothly and fully, keeping straight with rudder'.

After a few seconds, the rumbling ceased – we were airborne – I could fly – I was hooked – someone find me a Spitfire, quick! Of course, I did not then realise that take-off is really no different from using a urinal, just point and squirt; it is the rest of the flight that is the hard bit.

A few days before this, 'Batchey' Atcherley had said: 'If any of you, young fellows, ever find yourself in charge of one of the

Royal Air Force's aeroplanes it will be for one reason only. It will be because you are the best man in the whole world to be doing it.'

At that moment I was convinced that I was the very man they were looking for!

2

Taking the King's Shilling

IN OCTOBER 1942 my friend from UAS, Andy Simms, and I simultaneously received a command from His Britannic Majesty, Emperor of India and Defender of the Faith, to present ourselves at Royal Air Force Station, St John's Wood. This fiat was accompanied by an ominously one-way rail warrant. In Andy's case this proved sadly prophetic.

Had we been in a film we would have been flying Spitfires within a week, and if American we'd be immediately promoted to at least colonel, and awarded medals quicker than the ribbons could be sewn on our uniforms. We realised, of course, that we would have to be taught to fly, but we had not fully appreciated the formalities, seemingly totally unconnected with aviation, which had to be endured before we could actually get near an aeroplane. Many would be of a medical nature. Despite our having been examined several times, especially in our most private areas, the indignity would be repeated. This close interest in our genitalia caused wags to enquire if we were expected to f*** the Nazis to death. In addition, our intelligence and aptitude would be rigorously re-assessed, presumably in case one's wits had suffered some decline since they were last assessed. However, one was never tested for a serviceman's most necessary attribute – a wide-ranging sense of humour. In fact there was the airman's oft-repeated mantra: 'If you can't take a joke you shouldn't have joined'.

RAF St John's Wood turned out to be an assortment of luxury flats, although there was precious little luxury in evidence. This fiefdom, which also embraced Lord's Cricket Ground and, with nice irony, part of London Zoo, was known as the Air Crew Reception Centre.

Using the term 'reception' in that context today would invite intervention from the Trades Descriptions office. 'Reception' has connotations of a post-nuptial nosh, or at least some cocktails and canapés affair. At worst it involves a smiling girl behind a desk at an hotel. This could not be further from the truth. ACRC (popularly known as 'Arsytarsy') was a seething mass of bewildered, bemused and emotionally battered young men who accepted any ignominy or discomfort in the hope of becoming pilots, navigators or air bombers.

The human brain has the capacity to blank out particularly unpleasant experiences, which undoubtedly accounts for the fact that I have no recollection of the first few hours spent in this hell. I recall nothing until I found myself one of a crowd of maybe a hundred being shepherded, shuffling, by a coven of corporals into a sort of makeshift prison in Avenue Road, which consisted of a block of flats surrounded by razor wire. Those who have seen film clips of the Gestapo rounding up 'undesirables' will be able to visualise the scene.

The flats on three or four floors each comprised a big room, apparently dividable into two using a folding partition, two or three smaller rooms, and a fitted kitchen, plus what estate agents call 'usual offices'. What was unusual to us was that opening off the kitchen was a servant's quarter consisting of two tiny rooms plus a miniscule bathroom with a 'sit up' bath. There were around twenty folding iron beds in each flat, so the occupants of two flats made up what was laughingly called a 'flight' of about forty men (or forty bodies, as RAF-speak would have it). The block floors, we were informed, were to be polished to see-your-face-in perfection, and windows would be kept shiningly pristine.

We were to be under the command of a corporal, a bright

little cockney who, it was later discovered, was in real life a Smithfield porter who had presumably been selected for the task because he was used to dealing with meat in bulk. He was a DI (drill instructor), there being two kinds of corporals, DIs and PTIs (physical training instructors) – these latter allegedly being DIs who had failed their Ignorance Exam.

'Our' corporal made what was obviously the routine speech of the 'There's a hard way and there's an easy way' variety. He made it clear that there were the king, the prime minister, and the Archbishop of Canterbury, but for practical purposes we could regard him as all three rolled into one. He stopped short of claiming supremacy over the Almighty but inferred that we could regard him as about on a par.

We were issued with four blankets, two sheets, an odd sausage-like thing called a bolster, a cover for same and three yard-square 'biscuits', which formed a mattress of sorts. Each morning the 'biscuits' had to be piled at the head of the bed. Three of the blankets had to be folded in a special way and piled on top of each other separated by the equally carefully folded sheets. The fourth blanket had to be folded in a different way to allow it to be wrapped around the blanket/sheet pile to form a giant but unappetising layer cake. I kid you not when I say that the mathematical accuracy of the assembly was checked with a set square and ruler! I do not recall where the bolster went but the cover had to be spotless so one slept with the cover off, resulting in the bolster itself becoming a sticky mess of the Brylcreem with which we felt impelled to plaster such hair as the barber had allowed to remain on our heads.

We were issued with coloured badges, which apparently identified to which of the three squadrons one belonged. The reason, we found, was that there was one dining hall (actually an underground garage) shared by the three squadrons, so each squadron was allocated half-hour slots to stagger the mealtimes. Dividing us into squadrons and sub-dividing into flights sounded very airman-like, but clearly about as far removed from aeroplanes as it was possible to get and remain on the planet. Unlike today, when over central London there is a nose-to-tail stream of aeroplanes letting down into Heathrow, the only objects that went heavenwards then were barrage balloons.

The high point was kit issue. The clothing was straightforward enough: one was weighted down with shirts, pants, vests, socks etc, and to top it off a 'cap comforter' which was a sort of scarf (the wearing of which was prohibited since it was considered 'unairmanlike'). It could be turned inside out to make a rather fetching hat, but since the wearing of this was also prohibited mine remained unused until handed in four years later.

For the actual uniform, one stood before an elderly corporal, who looked one up and down and called out two numbers. Immediately, a tunic and a pair of trousers were thrown at one. The numbers referred to sizes – my tunic was 6 but my trousers were an astonishing 27! Despite this disparity, they were an almost perfect fit.

So laden, it was impossible to carry the final items, two pairs of boots, which had to be hung around one's neck by the laces; anyone requesting a large boot size drew ribald comments from the WAAF storekeepers. What were more troublesome were the 'accoutrements'. The 'Helmets, Steel', the two packs and the 'Bottles, Water, one' were obvious, but the purpose of the assortment of straps and buckles collectively known as the webbing was not. The only thing we could be sure of was that the brass buckles clearly had to be polished. This miscellany provided the first introduction to the permanent staff 'perks'. One or more of us would find that a small but vital part of the webbing assemblage was missing.

After the corporal had delivered a fearsome lecture outlining the dire consequences of such a loss, he would adopt a kindlier tone, saying that he just happened to have such a piece surplus, and despite such a transaction being highly illegal, for our promise of silence he would sell us the item at a price commensurate with the enormous risks he ran.

The possession of kit seriously complicated the morning bed protocol. For starters, one's greatcoat had to be folded a certain way and placed on top of the sheet/blanket 'layer cake'. All the webbing had to be displayed in a certain way with the brasses, like all our buttons, polished to a golden gleam. The smelly, camouflaged gas-cape had to be hung in a certain way with the steel helmet on top.

At the foot of the bed one's water bottle was flanked by one's spare boots. These, if they failed to replicate patent leather, would be described as 'filthy' or 'farmer's'. These epithets alliterated neatly with the inevitable epithet that preceded them.

An apparently vital element was the water-bottle stopper, it obviously had to be balanced on the shoulder of the water bottle, but to which side? Should they all be on the left or the right, or perhaps those on the left side of the room should be on the right and those on the right side of the room on the left... or was it vice versa?

Finally, the foot-end of each bed must be exactly in line with its neighbour.

All this had to be in perfect order by the time the corporal showed up and shouted: 'Standbyerbed!'

This was the only time the corporals would call a bed a 'bed', on all other occasions it would be referred to as a 'pit', delicately omitting the 'w' word that described what they constantly accused us of indulging in when occupying it.

This was just on ordinary days. On kit inspection days, every item of issued kit which we were not actually wearing – pants, vests, shirts, socks mug, cutlery, 'cap comforter', 'housewife' (needle and thread kit), brushes (boot, clothes and tooth), the whole works plus the scruffy paper 'deficiency chit', which accounted for items such as 'boots, knee, rubber' with which we were never issued. Each item was arranged in its proper place with millimetre accuracy.

We were classed as 'PNBs', i.e. potential pilots, navigators or air bombers and considered ourselves to be the social, sexual and intellectual superiors of gunners, wireless operators and flight engineers who followed a different recruitment route.

No one aspired to be a navigator or an air bomber. Everyone wanted to be a pilot. After all, small boys wanted to be engine drivers; few had ambitions to be firemen or guards. In any case it was the pilot who got the medal, and who had ever seen an air marshal navigator? We were subjected to the blandishments of a fatherly figure wearing the old observers' winged 'O' brevet (often known as a 'flying a***hole'), who would interview you and point out that a person of such high intelligence would be wasted as a mere 'driver, airframes', or that being an air bomber would enable one to personally 'Hit the *Boche* in the b******ks'. These entreaties invariably failed, so it was down to the various aptitude and other tests to reinforce the failure of those unfortunate enough not to be selected for pilot training, who would forever have to limp along on 'half a wing'. The Americans managed things much better, with all categories of flying badge being fully double-winged.

Although those not selected as pilots saw themselves as superior to the 'manual grades' of air gunner and suchlike, and definitely superior to all ground staff, the corporals saw no superiority in us whatsoever, invariably addressing us as a 'shower of s**t'. This epithet was, of course, forcefully prefixed, as were all their utterances, with the usual universal adjective. In fairness they were not habitually blasphemous. The Almighty was almost never invoked, but the act of procreation most certainly was. Whether as adjective, noun or verb, this one word was inserted into every order, remark or observation. Curiously, although the word had a copulatory connotation, it was never applied to the actual act itself, although, somewhat amusingly, a most delicate euphemism might be tautologically prefixed by the universal obscenity.

All this humiliation was apparently deliberately choreographed by a guy called Air Commodore Critchley, who apparently shared the corporals' view of us and believed, probably correctly, that desperate measures were called for, to prepare us for the rigors of airborne warfare.

His qualifications for the post were impeccable; his 'day job' was managing greyhound racing so, as someone once said, treating us like dogs came naturally to him. Had we known that he was only an acting air commodore, holding the temporary rank of wing commander and the substantive rank of pilot officer, we might have been less in awe of him.

Not that we ever set eyes on this august figure. The only authority figures we normally encountered were corporals. In fact, one gained the impression that the whole of His Majesty's Royal Air Force was run by corporals, a notion that subsequent experience showed was not far from the truth. These extraterrestrial creatures apparently never had any pre-corporal existence but had sprung from the ground from dragon's teeth sown by some latter-day Cadmus, in mirror-shining boots, clutching their clipboards. This theory was supported by the impression that they had little experience of life in the real world. A speck of dust on a boot, or a trace of polish on a button, was reacted to with the horror of an elderly spinster confronted by some unspeakable perversion (except that the spinster's exclamation would not be so adjectivally embellished).

As far as 'our' corporal was concerned, we came to realise that he was no more evil than the other DI and PTI corporals at ACRC, but even the evillest of these seemed positively saintly beside a third type of corporal – the SPs (Service Police). With their red cap-covers, SP armbands, Blancoed webbing and holstered revolvers, they oozed evil. If you can imagine meeting a traffic warden with haemorrhoids you will have some idea of what these creatures were like. They patrolled in pairs, slowly proceeding, peak-shaded eyes emanating hate. Most corporals nursed ambitions of reaching the heights scaled by such corporals as Napoleon or Hitler. SPs believed they had already done so.

One occasionally glimpsed a sergeant or even a flight

sergeant, but these were supposed to be even more terrifying than the corporals, so one tended to avoid any direct encounter. Officers appeared solely to inspect, criticise and harangue.

Actually, in retrospect one must have some sympathy with these men, almost all of whom must had once aspired to fly, who were, because of some shortcoming or other, condemned to see these pimply youths taking what must have seemed to them the path to glamour and glory. To those who, having for years sweltered in Mesopotamian deserts or Punjab plains, had at last achieved two measly stripes, seeing these ex-schoolboys achieve senior NCO status within months or (horror of horrors) be commissioned as officers in swanky, bemedalled uniforms, would be a bitter pill to swallow.

Normally, most people would hesitate to be beastly to someone shortly to be promoted over their heads, but these guys had presumably worked out that the odds were against them finishing up in the same unit, so making the risk of future retaliation small.

Now a word about officers, or the sort of officers we encountered at ACRC. As we would discover later there were worthy holders of the King's Commission, who ably and honourably carried out a variety of onerous non-flying tasks. However, most of the officers in recruit depots could not be so described. Actually, it was seemingly deemed sensible to employ intellectually inadequate officers in positions where they could do the least harm. The one who seemed to be in charge of us was particularly obnoxious, but to our delight had a name that was a homophone of a very rude word that summed up his character exactly.

Opinions differed as to the backgrounds of these idiots. Some said that they were commissioned because their fathers had influence; others said that their preferment was due to administrative error. There was another theory, based on the fact that many were short and overweight or thin and excessively tall, that Messrs Gieves and Moss Bros had, due to wartime conditions, to employ unskilled staff who occasionally mixed up the measurements, resulting in them being left with rejected uniforms on their hands. At the same time there were recruits whose dimensions were so abnormal that their clothing requirements were outside the scope of stores inventories; they were, therefore, commissioned and these reject uniforms sold to them at a handsome profit.

It must be understood that besides us callow new recruits were 'serving airmen'; men from ground trades who had been selected for aircrew training. They were instantly recognisable by their less than pristine uniforms, which in some cases were the pre-1936 'dog collars' (buttoned to the neck), sometimes with a long service inverted chevron badge. These chevrons were not worn by NCOs, so for a man in wartime to have served for three years without promotion suggest his talents were limited, or perhaps too good to be spared from some orderly room desk. Three years? After three *weeks* we felt we had been in for a lifetime. I think I once saw a guy with two chevrons – eight years! It was unimaginable – he was in the service when I was still in short trousers. It was possible to have three badges (a Chinese sergeant), a most improbable thirteen-year sentence – more than you got for manslaughter, a crime that some corporals tempted us to commit.

Serving airmen who were already NCOs had to cover their stripes with armbands during working hours, but woe betide a ranker recruit who failed to address them by rank. Uniform and badges apart, these chaps proclaimed their serving airman status by their over-use of the universal expletive. Being older and more experienced, some could be useful mentors, but most were contemptuously jeering with the constant mantra of: 'Get some [service] in' or 'Your numbers' not dry'.

As regards numbers, they were especially scathing about the seven-figure numbers of recent recruits: 'That's not a number, that's the population of China.'

The corporals saw the serving airmen as ready allies in their nefarious scams. The corporals, like the poor, were always with us, from the unearthly hour when their obscene shouting commenced until lights out. Then one morning an eerie corporalless silence was broken by one of the serving airmen reminding us that it was the corporal's birthday and that he would be greatly saddened if this anniversary were to be unmarked. Therefore he had taken it upon himself to make a collection and proceeded to extract sixpence from each of us. (Since we were theoretically on duty for 24 hours each day, sixpence represented four hours pay!)

The 'Ronson lighter scam' was run by the corporal himself. Although such things were unobtainable at the time, he produced a top of the range example in a presentation case. Apparently, it had been 'discovered' by a non-smoker who was prepared to raffle it (for 'charity' of course). We were 'invited' to purchase tickets for only sixpence, in support of some unspecified 'good cause'. A week or so later a brave soul would enquire as to the outcome of the draw. The corporal would assume a mind-casting-back expression before announcing that 'someone in C Squadron' had won it.

The great activity that seemed to take priority even over intimate inspection was haircutting. One only had to stand still for two seconds before some corporal would order one to have a haircut. (Just had a haircut? Well, have another!) As regards the cutters of hair, their grading was something that the RAF got right for once. There were five pay groups. Group 1 being the highest and Group 5 the lowest. Barbers were in Group 5, which was officially classed as 'totally unskilled'.

In reality, most of our time was spent in drill and physical training. The former entailed marching round the streets and the latter running round the streets.

As far as drill was concerned, my University Air Squadron experience had made me familiar with the rudiments. Now, I was moving into unknown territory. Take stamping and shouting, for instance. This was something the gentlemen cadets of the UAS did not do; they left that sort of thing to the College Home Guard. Now we were expected to make a frightful din. Again the dozen men in the UAS were one thing, but a hundred brought new challenges such as 'dressing', which was nothing to do with putting on clothes but was the arranging of men according to size. The idea was that on the march the big guys would lead so that the enemy would see them first and run away. As I saw it the trouble was that if the enemy just hid, then when the column had passed they would only see the small guys and think, 'They aren't all that big, let's attack them from behind'.

Of course, before marching off the men would have turned left or right to form a column. Magically the ranks became files and the files became ranks, not an easy concept to encompass. Anyway, while we marched around the streets of St John's Wood a problem with having all the tall blokes in the lead became apparent. They were liable to take longer strides than the little men at the back, with the result that the latter had to break into a trot to keep up. We found this amusing. The corporal did not.

We had approximately mastered all this and more, such as double marching on the spot (running without going anywhere), when we entered the arcane mysteries of the blank file. If you had ninety-nine men they made up three ranks of thirty-three, and when they turned they made thirty-three files. However, what if you had 100 men, or ninety-eight, for that matter? How did you get on? This is we discovered was the blank file. It works like this: if you are one man short when the parade is drawn up in three ranks, there is an imaginary man next to the end man in the middle rank. If you are two men short the same thing happens in the rear rank also. If the parade is ordered to about turn, the front rank becomes the rear rank, so the real man in that last but one file has to take two strides forward to fill the blank file in what is now the front rank. If this blank file was at, say, the right-hand end and the parade was turned right, the blank file (which was a blank rank) was near the back of the column. Should the opposite be the case this put the blank rank that was the blank file near the front, which would never do, so some fancy shuffling was required, the details of which now escape me.

If you think it was as much a waste of time reading this as it was writing it, think what a waste of time it seemed actually doing it!

Much of the drill involved the 'paying of compliments'. This did not mean telling people how nice they look but was a posh term for saluting. This was more complicated than just the basic 'longest-way-up-shortest-way-down'. One had to know how to pay compliments when riding a bicycle (eyes smartly right) or when in control of a motor vehicle (sit to attention) – indeed every eventuality was catered for.

One was supposed to salute officers of Allied and Friendly Nations. This proved difficult as an American private wore a better uniform and more medals than a British colonel, and a Belgian commander looked much like a bus conductor. The consensus was to salute everyone in uniform. Mercifully, we did not get involved in paying compliments when armed. Then one had to slap the weapon if the officer was of junior rank, and assume the present arms posture if of senior rank. The trouble was that a French *adjutant* (warrant officer) was indistinguishable from an Albanian admiral. In any case, as we would find out later, if a loaded Sten gun was slapped the whole magazine would be discharged.

Overarching all other activities was the thrice-daily queuing for food. The ramp down to the underground eating area was of smooth concrete, so as well as being boring it was actually a dangerous occupation. Since everyone had new nailed boots that failed to grip the steep concrete the queue became a phalanx of motionless men inexorably inching forward like an Alpine glacier, generating a suffocating crush at the entrance to the makeshift cookhouse.

The food was surprisingly good by wartime mass-feeding standards and, in fact, was praised by those who had recently escaped from the posher type of boarding school.

The act of feeding also gave rise to problems. Apart from the long time queuing and the short time allowed for eating, there was the problem of cutlery. Immediately on arrival we had been issued with a knife, fork and spoon which we carried about our person at all times. After use one 'cleaned' the cutlery by dipping it into a vat of filthy, but scalding-hot water. However, what did you do with a bunch of dripping wet and extremely hot set of 'eating irons'? We had six pockets, to use – either of the two trouser pockets would endanger one's vital organ but if any of the four tunic pockets were used they would protrude, causing apoplexy in any corporal one happened to pass. The result was that many went around clutching a handful of ironmongery. In addition one was lumbered with an earthenware mug which was hooked on the little finger of the same hand – the left hand, since the right hand was reserved for saluting purposes, and to salute with a hand carrying cutlery could cause serious injury.

3

No One Said it Would Be Like This!

THEORETICALLY WE WERE free from 17.30 hours (as we were learning to call half past five), but to protect us from the temptations of a wicked city a foolproof system of booking in and out was devised to ensure our safe and unsullied return by 22.30. Our flat block, like all similar ones, was surrounded by a high and dense perimeter of razor wire, with one tiny wicket gate guarded by a revolver-toting SP, who would let one in or out only if one produced a correctly time-stamped clocking-out card. This card was replaced in its rack after one clocked back in. The whole rack was inspected each morning and anyone whose card showed a clocking-in time later that 22.30 hours would be in deep trouble. This was also the case if one of the numerous SP street patrols stopped you and you failed to produce a correctly clocked-out card.

The scheme was virtually useless since it was not part of the gate SP's job to report late arrivals, and there seemed to be no check on the supply of blank cards. Thus, all one had to do was carry a card which was regularly time-stamped but never went in the rack, while one's official card never left the rack. That way not only could one return as late as one liked, but the pristine state of the card in the rack suggested that you spent your evenings staying in and assiduously polishing your kit. Despite our escape options, in reality we never had much time to go out. Boots and buttons had to be polished, webbing fittings had to be polished, the floor had to be polished, and shelves had to be dusted, then polished. Infuriatingly, however carefully the chores were done in the evening, by morning some speck of dust, some smear or trifling blemish would bring down the corporal's wrath.

It was said at the time that wars were started by armaments makers; we considered that they were started by the makers of Brasso, Cherry Blossom and Mansion polishes.

In addition to all this dusting and polishing, there was the taxing task of maintaining trouser creases. Unlike modern materials, where creases more or less look after themselves, keeping creases in woollen serge to the 'sharpen a pencil' standard expected was an ongoing chore. The kitchens of these ex-luxury flats had drop-down ironing boards (broken). Irons were available on a one-to-a-hundred basis, but these were either lost or broken. All one could do was smear soap inside the creases and sleep on them. Some put them under the mattress rather than on top, attaining a criss-cross pattern from the bed wires and no crease. Since soap was scarce one had to use it on one's trousers rather than one's body. However, on inspection one was looked at, not sniffed, so this did not matter.

If one did venture out it would be pitch dark, probably foggy. With almost no money one's scope was severely limited. There were the NAAFI, YMCA and other canteens, or one could be very adventurous and take a tube 'up west'. There was a certain piquancy about this, since we were liable to suffer dire penalties if we ventured beyond a certain radius; the whole of the West End was, apparently, well within this radius. On 3/- per day there was little to do except walk around and gape at the 'Piccadilly commandos' who then roamed the pavements of the West End. We all knew that there were women who would 'do it' for money, but few of us had knowingly seen one, let alone had one volunteer her services in graphic terms. For these few a lack of funds and the corporal's warnings of dire consequences ('It'll drop off, son and you'll have to sit down like a woman to piss') ensured that we did not take up any offers. There were, of course, official lectures on such matters, but they were so circumlocutory that it was not always easy to grasp exactly what we were being warned against. The corporal's warnings of consequences and vivid decryptions of the terrors of 'special hospitals' (based on personal experience?) were a far more effective deterrent.

Going 'up west' carried a more immediate peril than the pox – the Bakerloo Line. Bearing in mind that a fate worse than death awaited anyone who clocked in at 22.31, it was essential to catch a Stanmore train which went to St John's Wood and at all costs avoid those that branched off at Baker Street for Uxbridge. One waited on, say, Piccadilly Circus platform, gripped by cold fear, with the minutes ticking away as the next train indicator repeatedly showed Uxbridge. One evening I ran onto the platform just as the doors of a train were closing, totally failing to realise that there were a number of airmen in newly-issued uniforms not boarding. I got off at the first stop beyond Baker Street and found that I was at Finchley Road. I had to take a train back to Baker Street to catch a Stanmore train. I then had a breathless sprint from St John's Wood. By great good fortune the SP at the gate was a decent fellow and rushed me through (usually anyone arriving at the gate near 22.30 was liable to have his clock card and identity card scrutinised very slowly indeed, to try to ensure that he arrived late at the clock). I recall seeing the clock registering 22.30 as I frantically fumbled to get my card in the slot and hearing it being stamped a millisecond before the clock registered 22.31!

Whatever one did in an evening, the best entertainment was after the loudmouths returned and those with the most active imaginations let fly. These were the ones who had 'got lucky', invariably with some 'rich bitch' who was 'begging for it', and whose demands were both excessive and inventive. How anyone could imagine that, in a metropolis crammed with randy servicemen of every nationality, any female rich or otherwise would need to resort to supplication, I do not know.

Whatever the evening, it was overhung with the spectre of the morning to come. Besides the re-sweeping and re-dusting, there would be the precise alignment of beds and the aforementioned arrangement of kit. There were, of course, dilemmas. For instance, even after establishing the position of the water bottle cork (which was, strictly speaking, not a cork but a stopper, but then, the bottle was, strictly speaking, not a bottle but a metal container covered in felt), there was indecision as to whether the string should curl round the back or the front of the spout. But full? Did this mean literally full, or did one leave space in the top for the stopper? Eventually, we ceased such philosophical debates, having realised that whatever was done would be wrong.

Actually there was a more effective route to freedom than the fiddled clock-card – The Chit. I am sure that no museum or archive held a document that commanded such awe as a chit. With a chit one could go anywhere or do almost anything. One imagines that one could have entered Windsor Castle, ejected the king and ravished the queen if one had a chit.

I sincerely believe that had the piece of paper that Neville Chamberlain brandished at Heston airport actually been a chit, the Second World War would not have taken place.

Despite having almost the power of a holy writ, a chit was not an illuminated parchment, but a scrap of duplicated paper. Therefore, anyone with access to a typewriter and Roneo was in business. A typical chit stated that *Blank* was authorised to *Blank*, for the purpose of *Blank*, e.g. a funeral or Lodge meeting (Masonic references were particularly influential), or that *Blank* was excused boots or PT, or more or less anything. They would be signed and dated by *Squiggle* followed by an abbreviation of the signatory's rank. For forgeries the rank had to be carefully chosen. If the signatory was too junior he might be outranked and overruled; if too senior the authenticity might be questioned. The consensus was that squadron leader was the most appropriate rank. Thus, all these forgeries were signed *Squiggle S/L*. If the enforcers had been on their toes any chit signed by a squadron leader should have been subject to close scrutiny.

One man in our flight, elderly by our standards, had his own building firm so he would telephone requirements to his secretary, and the appropriate number of 'Overnight Absence', 'Excused Boots', 'Permission to Travel', 'Jewish, Moslem, Hindu (strike out as required) Excused Church Parade' or whatever the market was currently demanding, would arrive in the post next day (yes, next day delivery did happen then!). In fairness, his charges were modest and I believe he offered quite generous quantity discounts to his chain of distributors.

The skill at forging documents shown by aircrew prisoners of war must surely have been based on ACRC experience.

Films had made us familiar with airmen's talk – we could roll off 'Roger, Tally Ho and Wizard Prang' with the best of them. Despite this, here we found our vocabulary sadly wanting. Hitherto, to us a crime was an act of serious wrongdoing; however, we now found that a speck of dust in the wrong place was considered a crime. In fact, come to think of it, almost anything was a crime. There were, of course, degrees of crime, but the gravest was not murder or treason, but being idle. The service interpretation of 'idle' was pure *Alice in Wonderland*. Not laughing at a corporal's joke was idle, but not as seriously idle as laughing when the corporal *wasn't* joking. Quite a serious crime was 'behaving in an unairmanlike manner'. This was never defined but seemed to cover any activity or inactivity that displeased the corporal.

No corporal or other NCOs ever wanted to see your identity card: they demanded your 1250. They did not put you on a charge: they put you on a 252. Since every action was governed by a form it was less effort to refer to the appropriate form, the result being a conversation conducted in an arcane numerical code.

Pronunciation also had to be learnt. One did not wash in the ablutions but in the 'abol-lutions'. Men did not go on leave but on 'leef', or on a route march but a 'rowt march'. Property was recorded on an 'invent-tory', with everything having funny names, with everything plural, singularly being signified by the suffix 'one'. A toilet roll was 'rolls, toilet, airmen/airwomen for the use of, one'. Similarly, nothing was ever without something but was 'deficient of' so a broken mug would be: 'Mugs, drinking, china, airmen/airwomen for the use of, handle deficient, one'. Nothing was ever asked for, it was 'demanded', which seemed a most impolite way of making a request, but yes, a 'demand was put in for' every need. Presumably, if an airman wanted to have sex with a WAAF it would not involve sweet talk, soft, music or strong drink, but 'putting in a demand', although the lack of a suitable form would presumably cause problems.

Not that there was much likelihood of such a request being made by any of us. Turfed out of bed before dawn, marching, drilling and gymnastics in the street put any diversion requiring the expenditure of energy well down the agenda. In any case it would inevitably be met with a forcefully expressed: 'You've had it'. (Unless he was in possession of a chit?)

(I always was confused by this universal way of making a blank refusal. 'Leave? You've had it' or 'Second helping? You've had it'.

One had visions of the supplicant answering, 'But I haven't had it, I wouldn't be *** well be asking for it if I'd had it.')

I decided that learning to fly would be the easy bit.

Throughout all this I never really felt totally out of touch with home. We were paraded each morning in a certain side street opposite some rather tired-looking shops. On the fascia of one was the faded, once gold-leafed legend: 'Kerswell' – the name of a girl back home with whom I was acquainted. She proved to be the girl I married.

Eventually came the issue of flying kit, a plethora of gloves, socks, Sidcot flying suit and 'Teddy Bear' liner, big brown suede flying boots and, to pile joy onto joy, a real leather helmet and goggles. To round it off a 'frocks, aircrew' which was (or is, since I still have it) an enormous neck-to-knees woolly pullover. The flying boots were far too clumsy to walk in and proved not too good for rudder-bar purposes. As soon as I could obtain a proper leather pair, I gave these monstrosities to my father for his birthday. Unfortunately, the one good thing about them was their excellent insulation, with the result that he was unaware how close his feet were to the fire until the boots started to smoulder.

This flying kit was really exciting stuff. In the evenings we could dress up in it and dash about with arms outstretched, banking and weaving and making Biggles noises. Some who found the four-blanket issue inadequate at night welcomed the inner suit, the socks and even the gloves, to supplement their nightwear. However, no matter how enthusiastically the flying kit had been welcomed, the keenness waned when we realised that we were going to have to carry it!

There was one item of kit that was not welcomed. When one first staggered away from the Clothing Store, arms full of garments, boots slung around one's neck, there was, usually in one's mouth a 'deficiency chit', bearing the words 'Boots, knee, rubber, pairs, one'. Being a chit it was obviously a valuable document, so once the teeth marks had been smoothed out it was kept safely in a tunic pocket to be displayed only at kit-inspection. This was an occasion when all one's worldly goods, or at least the ones that His Majesty had been gracious enough to bestow upon one, were laid out on one's bed in a certain precise order as designated by a large photograph. Anything a millimetre out of place constituted a 'crime' and woe betide the perpetrator. What would have happened had an item been absent is best not dwelt upon.

Once a day a corporal would appear and call out names from his clip-boarded list. The named persons had to parade to surrender their deficiency chits and have their phantom rubber boots exchanged for the genuine article – bad news? Very! One was being consigned to Ludlow. No one knew where

Ludlow was but it was allegedly 'on the way to Wales' – which, in some eyes, was condemnation enough. Ludlow was also apparently some kind of labour camp where one lived under canvas and toiled in mud (hence the rubber boots). Officially, this was to toughen up those aspirants whose musculature was deemed 'deficient', but was strongly rumoured to be a building site owned by some air marshal, which would be sold at great profit after the war.

I was fortunate to escape this fate, but one fate that could not be escaped, even by possession of a chit, was drill, which overarched, as they say these days, all other activities. All this drill seemed pretty useless. Admittedly, marching in an orderly manner was clearly the most efficient way of moving a large body of infantry, but we weren't going to be infantry, we were going to be pilots, whom, as we knew from the films, moved around in MG sports cars with the hoods down, their scarves trailing. Failing that, they would be crammed into lorries, with parachutes shouldered, quipping merrily about giving Jerry a taste of his own medicine.

My UAS experience had made me familiar with the basic idea of 'getting fell in' (arranging ourselves) in three rows called 'ranks', which were nothing to do with that other sort of rank, for example sergeant or corporal. Being an alumnus of a UAS also entitled me to the dignity and status of a leading aircraftman, which gave me the right to display a propeller insignia on my arm. LAC was not a rank but a grade. Therefore, it conferred no right to issue orders to my propellerless colleagues, and any attempt to do so would be met with an invitation to do the anatomically impossible. You had to be at least a corporal before you could say, as Luke put it, 'Go and he goeth, come and he cometh'. However, this advancement did carry a pay rise of a dizzy 50 per cent (from 3/- to 4/6 per day).

Although I was automatically an LAC from day one, in the strange ways of the Air Force I could not be officially an LAC until this massive advancement had been gazetted in a

Personal Occurrence Report. PORs were wedges of duplicated pages that were issued daily and apparently no one could be promoted, demoted, upgraded, downgraded, receive a decoration, commendation or mention in dispatches, or just be posted to another unit without first being cited in a POR. It gave me quite a frisson to think that in every mess, every dining hall, every office and orderly room in Flying Training Command, crowds would jostle in front of notice boards to read that *AC2 Richards 1653043 to LAC w.e.f.* (with effect from) *18 10 1942'*. One could imagine this intelligence being radioed to Berlin by some spy in an attic, causing the Nazi High Command to wring their hands and exclaiming, 'Zee var iss lost!' Oddly, that same POR carried the announcement of Air Commodore Critchley's substantive rank being raised from pilot officer to flying officer, so I felt that I, by leaping over AC1, was fast catching him! If I could be raised two rungs up the promotion ladder in two weeks, I could be an air chief marshal by Christmas.

Whilst all new recruits seemed to induce contempt among the serving airmen, a recruit with propellers on his arms induced apoplexy. This was understandable as they would have sweated under a Mesopotamian midday sun to achieved AC1, so to have a smart-arse college cadet making LAC after 'five f***ing minutes' must have been riling.

4

From Limbo
to Limbo

MATTERS AT ACRC were geared to everyone being there for three weeks. There were three squadrons, each of which in turn emptied itself of recruits on a Friday, and replenished itself with a fresh batch on the Saturday. That was The System, and whilst one could insult the king and commit an indecent assault on the chief of the air staff with relative impunity, buggering up The System was not on.

However, bugger it up I did, since at the expiry of the three weeks I was confined to sick quarters with a bad inoculation reaction.

Sick quarters occupied several flats in an even posher block than the one in which I had been billeted. It was staffed by WAAF medical orderlies working under the supervision of the magnificently caparisoned officers of Princess Mary's RAF Nursing Service. Oozing competence, they acted rather like old-fashioned matrons on steroids, who, for instance, decreed that inmates must 'lie to attention' when either they or a medical officer was on the ward. For some reason they feared we might catch 'bron-chittis'; apparently we were allowed to perish from any complaint other than that.

In retrospect, I was lucky. There was another recruit who displayed similar symptoms; although he became a famous entertainer, he was dogged by ill health throughout his comparatively short life.

Although by apartment standards the rooms were spacious, they made small wards – I shared a two-bed ward with a charming man from Northern Ireland who possessed a fund of anti-Catholic jokes. I do not recall seeing any doctors, which possibly accounted for my speedy recovery. Since no doctor could be found to authorise my discharge I spent several days wandering around waiting for the next meal until someone spotted me and had me ejected from the premises with dire warnings about malingering.

There was just one day when the monotony was broken. A squad of men appeared, furiously cleaning and polishing. All patients were ordered back to bed and amid much cover-straightening told to lie still and stop talking. Seriously bored, I fell asleep. I was awakened by my wardmate getting up. He remarked that some old woman had been in and wished us a speedy recovery. It emerged that the 'old woman' had been Mrs Eleanor Roosevelt, wife of the President of the United States.

She had naturally been shown only patients with nice, non-contagious, above-the-waist ailments, but the story went around that she thought she had been visiting 'brave pilots' recovering from Battle of Britain injuries. She had visited the kitchen and tasted the food given to the patients. However, said kitchen had been one of the unused ones specially cleaned up for the purpose by cooks on loan from the Savoy. It was said that a bathroom had been set aside for her to 'freshen up' in, resulting in a rush by the WAAF orderlies wishing to 'share a seat', as it were, with the First Lady of the USA.

Having made good my escape, I returned to my old quarters to find it full of strangers, my intake being long gone, and there was no trace of my kit. Having had the effrontery to meddle with the rigid 'three weeks and off', I was a sort of administrative pariah, with nowhere to rest my weary head. I contemplated going home and trying my luck with the army or the navy.

Happily, I fell in with the very friendly Flight Lieutenant Wagner, who was a complete contrast to the other officers. He found both my kit and somewhere for me to sleep. To keep me amused he made me an assistant to his Orderly Room Sergeant. The ORS proved to be an affable Welshman who talked a lot about the English/Welsh divide.

'They've no culture see, take girls fr'instance, all they want to know is are they blondes or brunettes – don't give a bugger if they are sopranos or contraltos'.

I had so far met no actual anti-Welsh feeling, just ignorance. There were men who could not believe that my father was not a collier. Some men's knowledge of Wales was based on films and novels, and they even had difficulty in appreciating that we had telephones and motorcars. Indeed I had already met one lad who resolutely believed that in Wales pit ponies had their legs cut short so they could work in low tunnels.

So the ORS and I passed time by swapping stories about the ignorant English and rather reprehensibly provoking the very nice Flight Lieutenant by pronouncing his name as 'Vaargner', to evince his petulant response of 'Wag-ner, gentleman please!'

It was all too good to last. Eventually someone found out that there was a recruit who was not drilling, PTing and – shock horror – suffering no indignities whatsoever. Thus, I was seized upon and banished to Brighton.

I have no recollection of the train journey, only of being part of a small draft, being marched through the town in full marching order by a horrid little corporal. That meant we wore the webbing harness on which depended big pack, small pack, water bottle, steel helmet and gas cape all topped off by a gas mask tied to the chest. Like any serviceman I had my kit bag on one shoulder but as potential aircrew I had a second kit bag of flying kit on the other. It gave a whole new meaning to the term 'knackered'. The next shock was that we were not going to Brighton, an attractive seaside town with slightly naughty overtones, but to RAF Brighton, a somewhat different matter.

RAF Brighton was called Air Crew Disposal Centre, a title

redolent of chilling possibilities and therefore referred to as ACDC, an acronym that had yet to acquire a sexual connotation. It occupied the Metropole and Grand Hotels and was a sort of garbage can for people who, for one reason or another, had been relegated to odds and sods status.

I was there for three weeks; I have little recollection of what we did apart from climb up and down sixteen flights of stairs (I was in a room on the seventh floor and everything seemed to take place in the basement). I have little recollection of how we passed the day, possibly because, having been woken at 05.45, it was early afternoon before we were fully awake. We must have drilled and PTed and surely polished, since we had by now assimilated the recruit's motto: 'If it moves, salute it, if it does not, polish it.'

Unlike ACRC, the floors were bare boards, so scrubbing, not polishing was required. It was clear from the discolouration of the boards that in all these attic rooms there had been a carpet with a linoleum surround, in every room but ours the lino had totally vanished, in ours there remained one solitary, foot-square, torn – but highly polished – fragment

We had metal polish and boot polish but we had no lino polish. Both the Brasso and the Cherry Blossom had failed to produce any sort of results on this wretched fragment of lino so we felt ourselves to be in a dilemma. To me the answer was obvious: since this appeared to be the only vestige of lino in the entire building, in the interests of uniformity as well as expediency the fragment was thrown out of the window. Fluttering slightly, it landed in the street far below at the feet of a civvy gent, who clearly believed it to be some new weapon of terror dropped from a Nazi aeroplane. He stepped carefully around it and made a defiant skywards gesture with his umbrella.

Next morning we realised we had problems. Not only was the portion of linoleum clearly visible on the Promenade far below, but also there was a square foot of unwashed floor where the lino had been. There was no time to wash or even brush, so we standing rigidly by our beds for inspection had to hope for the best but prepare for the worst.

The inspection party arrived: 'our' corporal, a sergeant and an officer.

'Standbyyourbedsossifcerpresent!!!!' screamed the corporal.

Now in fairness we were starting to encounter officers who wore flying badges and in some cases medal ribbons, who had been given undemanding tasks as a rest from, and reward for, operations, but this fellow's left breast was devoid of embellishment.

He looked and he sniffed. The sergeant shouted 'Sah!' The corporal shouted, 'Sahroomandsixmenreadyforinspection.' Adding a second 'Sah,' just to be on the safe side.

The officer nodded, having apparently satisfied himself without even using his fingers that there were six of us, walked around closely viewing us each in turn, from cap badge to toecap. When he came to me my relief (that he was not paying too much attention to me) turned to horror realising that he was looking down, past me.

'Whet is thet?' he said in a soprano imitation of Noel Coward.

'Sahwhat'swhatsah?' said the sergeant in a strangulated screech.

'Laineooleum missing thar,' presumably deliberately mispronouncing the word to indicate his unfamiliarity with such a lower-class substance.

'In-vent-tory!' screamed the sergeant.

With a one-pause-two movement the corporal proffered a clipboard. 'Beds six,' the sergeant called.

'Bedssixsah!' the corporal echoed.

'Biscuits eighteen', 'Biscuitseitghteensah!' The same liturgy for blankets twenty-four, sheets twelve. The same mantra followed for bulbs, lighting one and fire extinguishers one, but when linoleum, pieces one was reached, there was just silence.

'Linoleum, pieces one!' The sergeant repeated, as if the lino was supposed to come to attention and answer 'Present sir!'

There was a pause then the corporal diffidently said 'Deficient, sir'

'What do you mean "Deficient", corporal?' squeaked the officer.

'There ain't no piece of lino! Sah!'

The sergeant sensing that the officer was in danger of straying outside his perception envelope intervened. 'Officer can see thaaat! Where IS the effer?'

The corporal, placing his face closest to the nearest face, which happened to be mine, screamed, 'AIRMAN! WHERE'S THE EFFING LINO?'

'I don't know, corporal,' I ventured

'Officer present, answer Sah!' growled the corporal

'Yes sir, corporal,' I murmured

'Any lino in your rouse?'

'No corporal,' I replied, hastily adding a 'Sir'.

'I suppose you've lorst the effing lot. Wheresit yer comes from?'

'Wales, corporal sir.'

'That effing well accarnts frit then, they don't have no effing lino down no effing coal mine.'

The Bowdlerisation of the F-word arose from the widely held belief that to utter it in the presence of an officer was a 'crime' although apparently the matter would be overlooked if the offender was handling a mule at the time.

I don't recall the outcome of that incident. Probably it was assumed that losing lino was just a Welsh trait for which due allowance had to be made.

I vividly recall clay pigeon shooting on the barbed wire entangled promenade. The high spot of this was to point a shotgun in a westerly direction, elevate it to about 45° and let off both barrels. If one got it right the pellets would drop on the King Alfred (KA) naval cadets doing PT further along the promenade, with luck catching them in a toe-touching posture.

We used to go swimming, sharing the Hove baths with KA cadets, who made it plain that they believed they risked catching some dreadful disease by sharing the water with scruffy airmen. We, in return, suggested that at the rate their ships were getting sunk, they should hone their swimming skills.

However, whatever the inter-service rivalry, it was nothing when compared with the inter-nation rivalry. Brighton also accommodated French Canadian troops. These Quebecois hard men included survivors of the Dieppe raid, the failure of which, and the heavy Canadian casualties, were attributed by them to British incompetence in reinforcing the French Canadians. In addition, they also blamed the RAF for not providing appropriate air cover at Dieppe. Thus for a British person wearing an Air Force uniform, Brighton was a war zone. I recall one evening in the lounge bar of the Old Ship when one of our number, a large lad from some recess of the Antipodes, saw two Canadians entering the bar. He suggested that they seek an alternative hostelry, and when they demurred, decided that a 'pre-emptive strike' was called for. With an alliterative cry of 'C**ksucking Cannucks', he decked them both, one with each fist. Regrettably, they were merely the leading pair of a whole double-filed platoon. A serious melée ensued.

It would be several years before I met Canadian soldiers en masse again. It was late at night on a near-deserted Victoria station. There were 10 or 12 of them, wearing Airbourne berets, drunk and singing rude songs. Tall, big-booted with big packs, they were a terrifying sight. Then one spotted me and pointed; they gave a joyous shout and came thundering towards me! I was petrified. Then I saw that they were women, military nurses and that their elation was not due to the sight of a victim, but, the sight of the Ladies sign, near which I was unwittingly standing.

After three weeks of this energetic inactivity, we did get to fly actual aeroplanes at what was miscalled Grading School. Grading presupposes gradations, but here there were none. Ten flying hours taking off from a snow-covered field in open cockpits in freezing January weather and you were either IN or OUT. 'Out' meant a flying career as a navigator or air bomber terrorised by your pilot's antics. 'In' meant that as a pilot you did the terrorising.

We were at RAF Booker, once a fashionable flying club that now had little fashionable about it, especially in mid-winter. We were cold in the air, we were cold on the ground, we were cold in bed, flying was spent resisting the cold. We had Sidcot flying suits and liners (we slept in the latter) over heavy, knee-length, white pullovers. We had leather gauntlets over woollen gloves, over silk gloves. We had sea boot stockings and fur-lined boots, and we plastered cold cream on our faces but in the open cockpits of Tiger Moths we still froze. We were supposed to go solo before the end of the course. However, in those weather conditions, few if any did so. I was thankful I did not; the instructor sat in front of you in training, and the thought of facing the arctic blast unshielded was too awful to contemplate.

Added to all this, on the ground we were in the charge of an evil flight sergeant. Up until this time we were used to suffering the whims of NCOs who realised that in a few months we would outrank them and made it their business to make our lives as unpleasant as possible. However, this man pushed the frontiers of frightfulness to previously unknown limits. What with him and the cold we did not care how we were graded as long as we could get out of there.

In the end I was not graded at all. Apparently, due to the mislaying of the form certifying my competence, or lack of it, said competence (or lack of it) was not officially recorded. Presumably the Grading School could have been rung, but then the information would not have been 'official'. Possibly a 'demand' could have been put in for a copy of the form but as that would have not been an original document it would not have counted.

This put the authorities in some kind of dilemma. Every 'Passed Grading School' person had to be pilot u/t (under training), a navigator u/t or an air bomber ditto. Therefore I, as a safe compromise was classed for administrative purposes as a navigator u/t.

By this point we were already familiar with the power of The Chit; now we were introduced to the power of The Form. Obviously, no large organisation can function without forms and in 1918 these had to be devised by the new RAF. I'm sure those charged with the task would have liked to copy the forms used by another air force, but at the time there was only one independent air arm, that of Finland, and they had only one aeroplane and one pilot, so presumably did not need forms. They could have used Royal Flying Corps forms, but as these were army forms they would, presumably, have included all sorts of stuff about horses and such, so apparently the RAF had to start from scratch. One imagines that forms were devised as and when the need arose and presumably were serially numbered. Form 1 was not an account of enemy aircraft shot down or of bombs dropped but was a *Return of Officers and Airmen Held In Open and Close Arrest*. By contrast, the form that carried the full mechanical history of an aircraft and was signed by the engineers and mechanics, and countersigned by the pilot, and stated that an aeroplane was in all respects ready to fly, and without which no aircraft *could* fly, was Form 700s. Apparently there were 699 forms pertaining to matters that took precedence over this most fundamental of activities.

Presumably if in 1940 the Luftwaffe had been able to find a way of destroying Fighter Command's Form 700s all the Hurricanes and Spitfires would have been immobilised.

Since no form or chit could be found to cover an ungraded gradee, I was regarded once more as a saboteur of systems. Thus now classed as a 'floating body' I was to be 'banged up' at

His Majesty's Pleasure until such time as it could be determined to which branch of aviation I was least unsuited.

My place of incarceration was RAF Heaton Park where thousands of young men were assembled to be formed into drafts to be shipped to Canada or Southern Rhodesia under the Empire Air Training Scheme or to the USA to train under the Arnold Scheme. The latter was eagerly hoped for, since tales were filtering back of lavish hospitality and of young ladies anxious to show, in tangible fashion, their admiration for the 'brave boys' of the RAF.

This transatlantic shipment took place on a vessel known as the *Louis Pasteur* – rumour had it that this vessel did not travel in convoy since its decrepit appearance made it seem so unlikely that it would complete its voyage that U-Boat commanders preferred to save a costly torpedo and let nature take its course.

Over the weeks and months others came and went, but since the branch of flying skills for which I was supposed to show aptitude was inscribed on missing documents, no one knew where to send me; therefore I stayed.

5

Marooned in Cottonopolis

HEATON PARK, MANCHESTER, was, and still is, a fine recreational resource while the sun shines, but on a wet winter's day, when one's sodden greatcoat was getting heavier and smellier by the minute, it was not. Some thousand men were corralled in the Park, while several times that number joined them during the day engaged in tasks of varying degrees of uselessness. This latter happy horde (which included myself), were released each evening to make their way to lodgings.

We 'outpatients' were billeted in private houses around Manchester and Salford. I was with nice people in Wiltshire Street, which was a sort of Coronation Street in Higher Broughton. They were always glad to let me share the fireside and the wireless during the evenings, but the husband could have bored for England. It appears that he was a Very Important Man – the Chief Refuse Collector for the whole of the City of Manchester. As such, he obviously went to work in a suit and wore a clean collar every day in case the Lord Mayor should wish to seek his advice on some matter of refuse collection. In the last war, he had apparently been some sort of orderly to General Allenby in Palestine and, according to him, the General relied heavily on him for advice. 'I said to him, "General, never mind what those fools on your staff say, why don't you march straight to Jerusalem?" And he said to me – "By God, sergeant, you're right."' As well as Mr and Mrs

Maskew there was the Old Lady, his mother. Anything anyone said, or anything on the wireless immediately reminded her of 'The Day Rochdale Town Hall Burnt Down'. Her descriptions of the flames rising to the sky, the ring of hooves on the cobbles as the fire engines arrived, the shining brass helmets of the firemen and the thrash and throb of the steam pumps, were dramatic stuff, but not when heard for the third time in an hour. How the delightful wife put up with the pair of them I will never know. I returned ten years later expecting to find her looking ten years older, but having buried both of them, she looked ten years younger.

It was not common for there to be only one billetee in a house and my landlord constantly told me how he had begged to have two, but his wife confided in me that he tried every way to avoid having any!

Amongst ourselves we swapped stories about billets. Most were in houses in terraces similar to Wiltshire Street, although some were grandly accommodated indeed and there were inevitably lurid boasts centred around husbands on night shift.

It cannot have been easy for the householders – a street of, say, sixty houses might have more than a hundred cuckoos in their nests, who, besides any disturbance they might individually cause, might unite to form impromptu Male Voice Choirs serenading the streets with regrettably explicit ballads.

Not all were as unfortunate as one family whose complaint dossier I 'happened' to read when on evening duty cleaning offices in Heaton House. It was from a householder in the street where I was billeted. These redbrick terrace houses had been four-bedroomed, but at some time one of the middle bedrooms had been converted into a bathroom with a bath and washbasin – no lavatory, that remained in the yard. The bathroom had the cold-water header tank tight against the ceiling. Apparently, the billetee found that the taps were dry. Being a handy type of lad, he had stood on the edge of the bath to inspect the header tank. It seems he lost his footing, instinctively grasped the tank, which came away, falling and smashing the bath, while he, devoid of support, also fell, demolishing the handbasin. The broken cold-water supply pipe then proceeded to flood the house, fused the lights and brought down ceilings.

Our 08.30 to 17.30 days were spent within the confines of Heaton Park, in the fine eighteenth-century Heaton Hall, and in the numerous temporary buildings clustered around where we were fed, drilled, instructed, inspected and generally kept out of mischief.

Some existing buildings were adapted. For instance, in at least one of the ladies' conveniences the customary cubicles were augmented with gentlemen's porcelain. This caused us some puzzlement, since although placarded 'Toilets, Airmen' the original 'Ladies' sign remained visible.

It was explained that Lancashire women adopted a masculine stance when attending to calls of nature. This allegedly originated in the cotton industry, where mill girls forfeited pay for every minute that they were absent from their posts. Hence they developed this skill to expedite matters.

As at ACRC, we were under the command of corporals but presumably because we were nearer attaining a superior rank they handled us with more delicacy. They marched us here, there and everywhere – usually around the Park, but at least once a week to Harpurey Baths. On the way the corporal revived the WWI custom of having us call out whenever the squad passed a shop with an unusual name. Thus passing, say, 'Postlewaite' on a facia, we would be urged to call out, 'Good morning, Mr Postlewaite, good morning, Mrs Postlewaite, good morning all the little Postlewaites'. To this annoying, but innocuous, mantra might be added some ribald speculation concerning the bedroom activities of Mr and Mrs P.

There were ditties too. Passing a well-endowed young

woman, for instance, the corporal would call out in time with the paces: 'Can-you-see-that-lovely-pair' and we would chant back 'Stick-in-out-in-to-the-air'.

There were all sorts of activities to fill the day but nothing was as frustrating as the use of the Bubble Sextant. We would be lined up on the tennis courts and at noon GMT we were tasked to find the latitude. Despite the fact that we were using the devices that today would be described as 'state of the art' we got results that varied from Birmingham to Carlisle, and were berated accordingly. Years later, I found that this was the sort of error inherent in these gadgets! Added to this the errors from operating, in the dark, in a bucking aircraft, possibly being shot at, it is little wonder that allied bombing was so inaccurate pre-radar.

All the time we were aware that we were living under the shadow of 'The Boat', which, like the Grim Reaper, would steal up on us unannounced at any time. We existed in a sort of mental sprinter's crouch waiting for the starting pistol.

As the days turned to weeks and weeks to months and the bite of winter turned to the breath of spring one sought ways of breaking the monotony. The best was unquestionably taking part in 'Wings for Victory' days. These involved being bussed to one or other Lancashire cotton town, then, in the shadow of tall, redbrick, chimneyed mills, marching around the town. We would be accompanied by the Home Guard, the ARP (Air Raid Precautions), ATC, WVS (Women's Voluntary Service), Boy Scouts, Girl Guides, Firemen, Bus Conductors, in fact anyone who could lay their hands on a uniform. We would also be accompanied by the conflicting cadences of several brass bands, the result being more of a slouching shuffle than a march. Nevertheless one felt one hell of a dog being cheered and applauded by the citizenry.

The intention was that this display of raw fighting power would persuade the citizens to put enough money into National Savings to buy a Spitfire (£5,000) or a Lancaster (£15,000). The bands, although depleted by call-up, were often famous and included the legendary Besses o' th' Barn Band. The star band was the imperiously-named Central Band of the Women's Auxiliary Air Force. It was based at Bowlee, which was a big RAF stores depot. Since many of the women were employed in relatively unspecialised tasks, they could select ex-professional musicians (Ivy Benson's Band formed the backbone) and thus create a band of a very high standard. The Drum Major, reputedly the tallest woman in the WAAF, was commandingly proportioned. Even more impressive than her presence was her dexterity with her staff, which she could twirl and toss in a way that would not have disgraced her Guards counterparts.

An ongoing task was to avoid the assault course which involved running, jumping, climbing, and swinging from ropes, as well as crawling through tunnels, traversing planks and casting oneself off precipices. Even dishwashing in the vast cookhouse was preferable to that. I know that nowadays people pay serious money to take part in 'adventure' courses, but with these there are safety precautions, one does not usually have horrible men shouting at you – nor do you have 'thunderflashes' thrown at you.

Thunderflashes were a sort of turbocharged firework that made as much noise as a hand grenade while being only a little less lethal. The sole attraction of going on the assault course was the possibility of purloining thunderflashes. These were useful for all sort of jolly japes, probably the most spectacular being to slip a sparking thunderflash into somebody's pack whilst it was strapped to their back – the rapidity with which a pack could be unstrapped and shrugged off never failed to astonish!

With the awful spectre of the dreaded assault 'curse' hanging over me, I volunteered to work at Bowlee. There I was detailed to report to a certain warehouse which turned out to be a huge, totally deserted structure stacked to the roof with boxed radio sets that left just a narrow gangway. On one occasion, craning my neck I glimpsed a wisp of smoke. Grasping a fire extinguisher I scrambled up the stack. I found that there was a huge void in the stack – occupied by numerous airmen smoking and playing cards.

For the most part, from 5.30 pm until 8.30 am, we were left to our own devices but occasionally duties would detain us at the Park. Such duties included guard duty, where one stood at the gate all evening and all night on a two hours on, two hours off, basis. I recall being on duty the night that the clocks went forward. I came off the midnight to 2.00 am turn only to find that the clock had leapt to 3 am, halving my 'rest'.

A more interesting duty was that of Fire Picket at the Hall. We were supposed to sweep each office, clear the grates and relay the fires. Since we would not have to light the fires the 'laying' was meagre, giving us time to go through files (this is how I learned the tale of the Billetee and the Water Tank).

These duties apart, having been ejected from the Park at 5.30pm, having eaten the last meal of the day we were at a loose end. One could return to the billet but my landlord's improbable tales of fighting 'Johnny Turk' and criticising my choice of friends (mostly old school friends) soon palled. I was never one for pubs, and cinemas made serious inroads into our meagre pay and involved endless queuing (we had enough of that at mealtimes). There were more robust spectacles such as the wrestling at Belle Vue Gardens. These had a distinctly forces slant. A huge man billed as a sergeant of the Military Police might be matched against a near midget described as an Aircraftman. The 'Aircraftman' would allow himself, amongst boos and catcalls, to be thrown, pummelled and jumped on – the referee blind to the most outrageous fouls. Then, suddenly the little man would seize the big one in a contortionist's lock and amongst resounding cheers, have his opponent screaming for mercy. Most nights there would be one wrestler who had 'killed' so many opponents that he had to wear a mask and use a false name. He would usually finish up prone and apparently lifeless.

The most cost-effective entertainment was to be found in the main streets of the city centre, where young women paraded in giggling gaggles. The drill was to target a group whose numbers matched one's own contingent. When all were paired off came the tricky bit – the 'split' – with the aim of separating the pairs. That achieved, one could get down to some serious smooching. Since in that era 'prohibited' areas were invariably extensive and strictly enforced, it was all very tame by today's standards.

Sundays presented a dilemma. One was not required to attend at Heaton Park, but the Park was the only source of free food. With no trams or buses, I regally tarried in my bed until my landlady indicated that she wished to make it. I then walked the couple of miles into the city, to that cornucopia of gastronomic delights, the Catholic Women's League Canteen in Mosley Street. I'm sure that the Women of the League did more to further the Roman cause than a whole conclave of cardinals ever could. Their double cheese on toast (twice) was a Sunday morning breakfast fit for an Emperor.

I met friends and we somehow amused ourselves, rounding off the day taking afternoon tea in the Midland Hotel.

Slowly the days passed, occasionally enlivened by persuading passers-by to form a queue for a non-existent bus, calling out to lorry drivers and pointing to a back wheel and scampering away when he stopped to look, or starting a rumour that the *Louis Pasteur* had been sunk and that we would die of old age at Heaton Park. This I half believed myself, since no one seemed to have been there longer than I had. Ominously, I started to get leave, admittedly only weekend passes, scarcely worth travelling all Friday night and all Sunday night for, but clearly an indication that I would not be going anywhere soon. Despite my pathetic performance with the bubble sextant, I was resigned to accepting my fate and volunteering to be a navigator – I would have volunteered to be a latrine attendant to get out of there. Then, after almost five months of this stagnation, at the end of the day I thumbed a lift on a lorry back to Higher Broughton. I was joined by another lad who apparently had been detailed to the Orderly Room. He gave me a garbled account of how some lost documents had been found for some fellow they had forgotten all about and that he would not have to wait for a boat but would be sent on a special pilot's course at once.

Thus it was that within twenty-four hours my landlady had kissed me in a tearful goodbye and I had a pick-up truck to Piccadilly Station all to myself. I was bound for No 21 EFTS (Elementary Flying Training School) to be taught to FLY!!!

6

Flying, and a Forces Return from Fordhouses

NUMBER 21 EFTS was situated in the suburbs of Wolverhampton and had developed out of Wolverhampton Aero Club. As at Booker, the Tiger Moths were civilian-maintained. The RAF element comprised cooks, clerks and some Service Police of unspeakably evil intent. For the first time I found myself in an almost corporal-free zone.

The excellent ground instructors were led by the colourful J. Rivers Oldmedow, the chief ground instructor, who could deliver an hour's lecture hopping, crutchless on his one leg. The flying instructors were a curious amalgam of older men who had been aero club instructors, pilots being 'rested' following operational tours. and recently-qualified pilots whose aptitude had singled them out for instructional duties.

The trainees were odds and sods who, for one reason or another, had not fitted into the mainstream Empire Air Training Scheme, Some were indeed very odd sods: Mourrisey, an Australian who knitted his own socks; Rigby, a suave Anglo-Brazilian, and Bonner, a gnarled Glaswegian ex-air gunner, who had been a prisoner of war in Ethiopia. He and the rest of his crew had been lodged in the Royal Palace, the officers in the quarters of the Duke of Aosta, the Italian Governor, while the NCOs lived with the staff. He spoke of trying unsuccessfully to enrage the duke's pet lion in the hope that it would attack the duke when he tickled its mane.

There was also Eaton, a cultivated Canadian who always had otherwise unobtainable nylon stockings for sale, apparently sent to him by his department-store-owning family; Bedford, a quiet tow-haired Yorkshire lad straight out of school; Brown, a faintly camp dress designer; Scoffins, a dour Midlander and proselytiser of political views that condemned Trotsky as too right-wing; Pettit, the son of an air marshal, who had the looks and hauteur of a Roman consul; Cheney, a Frank Sinatra look-alike; Cohen, a wise-in-the-ways-of-the world Londoner, and Bowry, who was later to be a pioneer of the then yet-to-be-invented helicopter. There were others, not vividly remembered except for the Turks, who regarded both our aeroplanes and their own lives as equally expendable. The presence of the Turks was due to the then ongoing charm offensive intended to thwart Nazi Middle-eastern ambitions. It was considered that if we offered free training to their pilots, Turkey would join the Allies.

There was one snag. Except for the Turks, we were all in one long hut. Having spent the previous four months sleeping in solitude in the Maskew's back bedroom, this took some getting used to. This was exacerbated by a noisy element who regularly woke the more sober-sided men when they returned from an evening pubbing in Wolverhampton. They compounded the nuisance by playing the radio at all hours (until someone poured a mug of tea into it!).

I became quite friendly with Bedford, who was both a gentleman and a gentle man. He had an unswerving loyalty to the Co-operative movement and would go out of his way to buy even the smallest purchase at a Co-op shop. Invariably, when asked for his dividend number he would tell the assistant to use his or her own. When I asked him why, he said something to the effect that he would not be around to collect the 'divvy'. I assumed that he meant that he would not be in the area when it was paid. Later, I was to wonder if he meant something quite different. He was very much a non-drinker, so it was a great surprise when one evening, he went into town with the boozers. He came back roaring drunk, brandishing a knife, and attempted to attack me. Next morning he had no recollection of the matter, but he did have a monumental hangover. This ensured that henceforth he ventured no further than the NAAFI.

The Tiger Moth, a stick-and-string biplane, had, and still has its adherents, mainly because however well you fly it, it can always be flown better. For us, the challenge was to fly it at all. We had all flown in them or been flown by them at Grading School but this was different: this was now for real. Plus, it was springtime and the air when aloft was invigorating rather than tortuous – one felt one could almost see the Wall of China and the weather was one's friend. Between flights one could lie on the grass and savour its freshly-mown smell mingling with the hot oil smell of Gypsy engines and pretend that one was a privileged member of some exclusive flying club. The gracious living aspect was heightened by the canal behind our flight where narrow boats intently chugged and at weekends couples canoodled in hired skiffs. It was not quite Henley Regatta, but close enough for us. Although there were no waiters to bring you cooling drinks, there was the YMCA van. Although, unlike its RAF Booker counterpart it was not driven by an almond-eyed Albanian Princess (exiled King Zog lived nearby), it was stuffed to the roof with rare delicacies such as Eccles cakes, parkin and Bakewell tarts.

Comestibles aside, the job in hand was to learn to fly. The first great hurdle was the first solo, which, to paraphrase Winston Churchill's then recent speech, was not the end of training, nor was it the beginning of the end of training, but was the end of the beginning of training. I did have problems. Taking off was easy: you pointed the thing the right way, opened the throttle and by the grace of God and the courtesy of Messrs de

59

Havilland you were in the air. I could do it with my eyes shut – and sometimes did.

Going around the circuit was easy, but landing was a different matter. It required some judgment to position oneself and make a nice descent towards the appropriate point of touchdown. One then eased back the stick, closed the throttle and, while trying to hold the machine clear of the ground, allow the speed to decay and the plane sink gently to the ground. The snag was that this had to be commenced at exactly the right height.

I had some difficulty in judging this. For reasons of leave, sickness and postings I seemed to have had a different instructor each day, all with different ideas as to how to make this judgement of height.

I was haunted by what Wing Commander 'Batchey' Atcherley had said to one of the University Air Squadron cadets who had asked why we did not have tricycle undercarriages like the Americans.

'Why?' said Atcherley?

'Because they are easier to land, sir.'

'Land?' thundered Atcherley, 'LAND? Americans may need aircraft that are easier to land, but let me assure you boy, a pilot in the Royal Air Force is adept in every sort of manoeuvre, so certainly is in no need of any assistance whatsoever on such a routine matter as landing!'

I then had the good fortune to be allocated to a Sergeant Picot, a small, likeable young man. Although his home was in Nazi-occupied Jersey, he did not rail against his misfortune of being denied an operational appointment, but got down to things. His only party piece was the ability to find where the Birmingham Canal followed the contour on the side of a valley, and to drop down to below canal level and wave to a bargee. This was mild when compared with some of the younger instructors – one attempted to demonstrate his talent for Fleet Air Arm deployment by trying to land on a speeding bus. There was talk of another who repeatedly flew very low over a potato-picking party of Italian prisoners of war, until he was brought down by an energetically whirled, part-filled, bag of spuds! Surely this was the only instance of an EFTS Tiger being felled by 'enemy action'.

Picot, on the other hand, buckled down to the task of getting me off solo. Despite relying on a 'by guess and by God' method of judging landings, I eventually made a couple of good ones. He directed me to taxi in but keep the engine running. He then extracted himself from the front cockpit and was replaced by the flight commander, with whom a couple of taciturn circuits were completed before he in his turn got out to be replaced by – nobody! I recall the trepidation of seeing him securing and checking the front-cockpit harness before lightly springing to the ground with a pat on the shoulder and a nonchalant: 'Off you go, son'.

It took some time to realise that I was now supposed to fly this thing, up in the air – on my own!

With most tandem seat aircraft the instructor sits in the back so you can always pretend he is there when he isn't. With a Tiger the instructor sits in the front so, particularly on the first solo, one is only too aware that where there used to be reassuring shoulders there is just a void.

I recall it as being a perfect afternoon. In a gentle breeze I taxied out unaided, turned until I was exactly parallel with the idling windsock and, aiming at the distant Wrekin, very tentatively opened throttle. Relieved of an instructor's weight, the machine leapt into the air taking me unawares.

As I went round the circuit my anxiety about landing grew. I decided that as long as I somehow made contact with terra firma (the more 'firmer' the less terror), even if I totally wrecked the aircraft I would have achieved my life's ambition of flying an aeroplane. In the event my landing was perfect. When I taxied in, Picot congratulated me on the landing and asked why I had not done a few more, but I knew when a fluke was a fluke.

The next day Picot was posted off to train for more martial

aviation. Whether this was co-incidence or as a reward for getting me off solo, I shall never know. Normally, it was a serious setback to change instructors at this stage – in my case it might have proved disastrous but in fact it was the reverse.

I had, of course, seen my elderly shambling, grotesquely overweight and permanently-out-of-breath new instructor, whose Black Country accent was so thick that he was almost unintelligible. His vain attempts to close the zip of his filthy Sidcot flying suit made him look like an unsuccessful attempt to wrap up a parcel in a coalhouse – I later learned that as an ex-locomotive fireman, he wore his flying kit when moonlighting on the footplate at night. He rode an old, tiny motorcycle that his overhanging bulk rendered all but invisible. Enveloped in a cloud of smoke, he appeared to hover along the road held up by some supernatural, but very noisy, agency. This was Sergeant Wild. I assume that he had a Christian name but to all, including his pupils, he was 'Tubby'.

More than once in later life when being interviewed for a flying post I have been asked if the Sergeant Wild in my logbook was Tubby Wild of Wolverhampton. When I replied that it was, I was immediately told that the job was mine.

The term 'gifted' fails to encompass Tubby's ability as an instructor. Educationally, intellectually and probably socially limited, he clearly had had a struggle to master his craft. This gave him an ability to understand a learner's problems in a way that natural flyers never can. His conversational skills were limited, but he could communicate most effectively by means of skilfully modulated adenoidal grunts. This way he could convey disappointment at any shortcoming, and you strove and strove to do better.

As regards landings, these days one has simulators. Then, we only had Link Trainers. Excellent though they were, they were no help with landing. Tubby eschewed the traditional 'fifteen feet' or the 'wait until you can count the blades of grass'. Instead he called upon the assistance of the Mayor, Aldermen and citizens of Wolverhampton. He had discovered that a passenger in the upstairs front seat of a double-decker trolleybus is at exactly the correct height to commence the landing procedure of a Tiger Moth. I was therefore told to board such a vehicle at the Fordhouses terminus, take a 1½d Forces Rate Return to the town centre and to repeat the exercise until I had a permanent mind's eye image of the road ahead from that top deck front seat.

The next time I flew with him I made a perfect 'daisy cutter'. The fact that I went on to make some 5,000 perfect (well, almost all perfect!) landings, in everything from a glider to a fast jet, over the next sixty-three years is surely a tribute to his system.

Under Tubby's patient guidance one could enjoy open-cockpit flying, seeing, feeling, hearing – plus, unexpectedly, smelling. Besides the engine-smell and smell of new-mown grass on the ground there were smells in the air – the sooty whiff of a dirty chimney, the woody scent of a bonfire. On a still, warm day one could even detect the tang of tar on a fence being painted, oil paint, or even a farmyard muckheap. These transient treats were lost when one progressed to Perspex enclosures.

For the next six weeks I blossomed under Tubby's gentle chidings at the slightest sign of ham-handedness: 'Imagine you're tickling a trout', or, 'Planes are like women: you never get anywhere if you try to rush them, you have to gently persuade'.

Tubby was a wonderful man whose life was sadly cut short by illness – probably because someone was required to give refresher courses to the angels.

After you mastered all the manoeuvres, the next best thing was solo cross-country, where your aim was to find your way to, and land at, a strange airfield (in my case, Sealand on the Wirral). One would park one's aircraft, pretending that it was in fact a new secret fighter cunningly disguised as a Tiger Moth, and with your goggles on your forehead, nonchalantly stroll in to report, stating that you have come from Wolverhampton, attempting to pronounce it so it sounded like Vladivistok or somewhere exotic. Actually, I did rather better than one chap, who, seeing a big hoarding: 'VISITING PILOTS TAXI HERE' took it too literally and ran into it, collapsing the hoarding on top of his aircraft.

Eventually, under Tubby's inspired teaching I did master, adequately if not perfectly, at least those skills required from the beginning of take-off until the end of landing. I comforted myself that no one outside the genius bracket has ever been happy taxiing a Tiger Moth.

The trouble was that although one could see ahead in a flying attitude, tail down on the ground the Gypsy engine, although a puny power unit, was very effective at blocking one's forward view, so when taxiing you had (and still have) to weave from side to side to see where you were going.

Unlike the steerable nose wheel and/or differential brakes, we had no brakes at all. You were totally dependent on the rudder to change direction, but a rudder does not work unless air is passing over it. If taxiing into wind the natural breeze, combined with the modest slipstream necessary to slowly propel the aircraft, gave sufficient control so that one could proceed in a nice steady zigzag. In a crosswind things were very different, since the machine constantly strove to 'weathercock' into wind and this could only be countered by using brisk bursts of power. Taxiing downwind was even worse since the slipstream had to overcome the wind before it could even begin to influence the rudder. Thus a lot of power was required and this was liable to make the machine gather excessive speed, usually towards another aircraft or other object, which meant that even more power was needed in order to change direction – a procedure which was liable to end in the air or the boundary fence.

Fortunately, we used an all-grass airfield since taxiing on concrete, where the tailskid provides little resistance, is something else again. Years later I found that taxiing downwind, even on the gentlest of slopes, was impossible – there was little chance of steering and no way whatsoever of stopping. One's only hope was to switch off, leap out and firmly grasp a strut and try and turn the plane across the slope. The trouble was that then it would weathercock until it was facing uphill and into wind, whereupon it would begin to roll backwards.

The only way to taxi in a strong wind, even on grass, was to have attendants holding each wingtip. So it was laid down in SSOs (Station Standing Orders) that a gesture by a Tiger Moth pilot to any passer-by was a direct order to go to his assistance.

The perimeter track was constantly patrolled by a pair of bicycling Service Police slowly pedalling in exact synchronization, circling the airfield like hungry vultures. Thus, if such a pair were spotted, whatever the wind, they would be directed to abandon their bicycles and man each wingtip as far as the opposite side of the airfields. Invariably when they had trudged all the way back to their abandoned bicycles another pilot would signal that he was having 'difficulties'; with luck this could be kept up all afternoon.

Somehow, we all found that we had demonstrated that we could locate and land at a distant airfield and find our way back again. We could do aerobatics (well, sort of), we could fly in formation, we could 'recover from unusual positions' (a description subject to much ribaldry), we could do forced landings, precautionary landings, do steep turns, recover from spins and fly under an igloo-like tent relying solely on instruments. We and the examining instructors had survived the final handling test.

In short, we were the bees' knees, especially as all this was achieved with the loss of only two aircraft, the one crushed under a large signboard at Sealand and one landed short by a Turkish gentleman who burst through the boundary hedge to appear on the airfield minus wheels and wings.

We felt we would need little further training, we were competent to fend off anything the Nazis could throw at us, fit a machine gun to a Tiger and we could down Messerschmitts by the bucketful. Then came the occasion of the sorting of the men from the boys – night flying!

The first night solo was different from the first solo in daylight. It was frightening but not as frightening as the second night solo, since by then you knew how terminally terrifying it really was, particularly as the flare path was laid out so that one's landing approach took one past a very tall unlit, and hence invisible, chimney.

All along, Tubby's dictum had been that you never know when an engine is going to fail and if you've only got one to start with, you've got a problem, so always keep scanning the ground for suitable fields, so that when your engine lets you down (as one day it surely will), you will already have picked a field to land. Scan the ground? Cast into utter darkness, you did not know which way was up, let alone down. Anyway, how could we land it? Being high summer, the trolleybuses finished before dark, so how could we practise?

Even if the trolleys ran after dark, they had headlights. Proper aeroplanes had landing lights. However, devoid of an electrical system, Tigers did not. All they had were flares on each lower wingtip, fired by pulling a string. We did not use them, as when the ignition string was pulled they usually failed to light. If they did happen to light, they would probably set fire to the aircraft. Even if they did not they were likely to burn out just as one was about to touch down.

Initial take-off was OK, one merely kept parallel with a row of 'gooseneck flares', which were basically watering cans full of paraffin with flames coming out of their spouts, but after one passed the last, one was propelled into a darkness that totally redefined stygian. One then turned left and left again and looked for a row of lights. With a strict blackout in force these should have been easy to spot, but railway stations and marshalling yards had rows of lights and Wolverhampton was a railway centre. All one could do was to try to find the row that were flickering. Even when one had correctly located the flare path, made a correct approach and a good (ish) landing, one was uncomfortably aware how close the flares were to one's canvas wings covered with highly inflammable dope, not to mention the 15 gallons of petrol just above one's head.

It all seemed very odd that after a couple of months we were expected to night fly, while sparrows, a species that had been flying for thousands of years, never even attempted it.

Anyway, we completed the statutory night hours and indeed went solo, more because the instructors refused to risk their lives further than as an endorsement of our competence.

Following a final test flight we were all adjudged to have passed and free to libationally celebrate the fact.

EFTS had one last sting in its tail. The following morning, as we assembled in varying states of incapacity ready to be bussed to the station, it was found that several of us, including the most enthusiastic celebrants of the night before, were an hour or two short of the statutory eighty. The rest of us, therefore, had to wait while those pilots, having been assisted (or in one case, carried), to the aircraft were chauffeured around the sky by instructors until the necessary time could be logged.

7

Within the Hallowed Halls

WE KNEW THAT we would be moving onto No 17 SFTS (Service Flying Training School) at Cranwell in Lincolnshire. What we did not know was this RAF college, which had been closed at the outbreak of war, was being 'kept warm', as it were, by pretending to be an ordinary SFTS, substantially staffed by retainers striving to maintain pre-war standards. Guys who had spent a couple of decades building up traditions that had taken Sandhurst more than a century to develop were determined to hold on to those traditions.

For starters, we were housed in the magnificent college building, which had been slightly marred by an aircraft having crashed into its roof.

Having spent recent weeks enduring communal accommodation and being harried by Service Police, we were quite unprepared for the whole air of gracious peacetime living. For me the culture shock was heightened, when proceeding to Cranwell, by having found myself benighted at Peterborough and, through the courtesy of some footplate men, having slept in the London & North Eastern Railway section house used by train crews on 'lodging turns'. This was an unique experience for a non-railway person, but since my bed had all the signs of having been recently vacated by a fireman who slept in his overalls (and boots?), it made me thankful that I had not succumbed to early ambitions to be an engine driver.

At Cranwell we dined in a fine mess hall (no need to carry eating irons). The college band still played in the minstrel's gallery at dinner on Wednesdays, apparently unaware that 'dining in nights' were no more. This luxury was not always appreciated, and gave rise to comments that they should practice elsewhere.

The other distractions from eating were the paintings. As part of the dispersal of the pictures from London galleries a number had been loaned to the college, and were hung in the dining hall. In addition to portraits of the great and the good, there was one enormous canvas of a 'sporting bag' – a several times life-size depiction of a pile of dead deer, hares, birds and other unfortunate creatures, which did not aid digestion.

Admittedly, we were crammed two to a room in bunks, but we had the share of a servant who made our beds, cleaned our buttons and boots and, above all, polished the floor and called us 'Sir'. I shared with Cheney (no first name stuff here!), a rather reserved lad who had been trained in the USA under the Arnold Scheme. He had been sent home when the American doctors diagnosed a serious medical condition. His mother, the Matron of a London hospital, used her connections to have him examined by the best specialists in the country who pronounced him fit – hence he was at Cranwell to continue his training. Sadly he died of natural causes only a few weeks after completing the course.

In addition to the white cap flash we had worn since ACRC we now had white armbands, which marked us out as 'gentlemen cadets'. It was rather nice to have the local civilians step off the pavement when we approached – that is, until we discovered that it was widely believed that the armband denoted that we were suffering from venereal disease.

At Cranwell the oddities from Wolverhampton were augmented with a most unlikely mix of administrative misfits. These included a Leading Seaman who wore an RAF battledress with a rating's shirt and cap, who was obviously well connected;

he allegedly was related to Anne Boleyn. There was a swarthy Greek-Cypriot and an equally swarthy Egyptian. There was a French *adjutant* (warrant officer), who dripped gold braid, and a Dutchman who had been an officer in the Dutch Air Force: when captured in 1940 he had (with the knowledge of the Dutch Government-in-exile) joined the Luftwaffe and in due time was posted to the German Embassy in Madrid, from where he scarpered to Gibraltar with a wealth of intelligence. Understandably he was detained in Gibraltar until his bona fides could be established. While incarcerated in the naval gaol he learned English from his fellow inmates – hence his language was somewhat colourful. In addition we still had our Turks. Segregated at Wolverhampton, they now mixed with us, and a grand lot they were. Most had a good working knowledge of formal English but all were anxious to learn colloquialisms. They had apparently been issued with a list of 'banned' words, but we were able to teach them some expressions that had escaped the official list.

This assemblage of nationalities did give problems of address. Canadians and so on were 'Empire Colleagues' (not, repeat not, Colonials), the French and such like were 'Gallant Allies'; the Turks, being neutral, were 'Friends. When later the Italians changed sides they had to be called 'Co-belligerents'. All this was most confusing.

There were no Americans in the college but there were a handful around. They were all female officers, tall as trees, immaculately uniformed and impeccably groomed, attending one of the many training units that clustered around the college basking in its reflected glory. Since they all wore two medal ribbons one had the impression that these 'Gallant Allies' were actually gallant. I once was so bold as to 'chuck one up' (give a salute) and asked about the medals. They acknowledged me in the usual American way of touching their foreheads with a thumb and shooting out the hand as if about to give a Nazi salute then thinking better of it. They said that one was for being in the army, and the other for being in the 'Yurrupean thee-ater of apperations'. Since they were in uniform and over here the medals seemed superfluous. When I said as much, they reminded me that they were 'lootenants' (which sounded as if they were renting a lavatory), and assured me that they intended to 'make themselves worthy of the trust that their country had placed in them by awarding them their decorations'.

One of the first tasks we faced was being separated, sheep and goats fashion, into 'singles' and 'twins'. The former would train on Miles Masters, the latter on Airspeed Oxfords. Although we did not realise it at the time, it was a rather grim business since the 'singles' would go onto fighters and hence probably live, while the 'twins' were likely to go onto bombers and so would probably die. Back at Wolverhampton Tubby Wild had remarked that I had all the attributes of a good bomber pilot, inferring that I lacked the élan required for fighters. In the event aptitude seems to have been ignored and the selection was made purely by age, the callow straight-from-schoolers like me going onto singles and the old men pushing thirty being put on twins.

Although we 'singletons' had had our life expectancy dramatically extended we did not see it that way. The Oxford seemed as reassuringly safe as a club armchair, while the Master with its cranked wing and intimidating stance, seemed like a bruiser spoiling for a fight. Our fears were not entirely groundless. Empire Training Scheme pilots progressed from Tiger Moths to Harvards (the North American Aviation Harvard T-6) and only after a couple of hundred hours on this pussycat of an aircraft, did they face the Master. The Americans had it even easier, as after the PT17 Stearman, a heavier aeroplane than the Tiger, they went onto Vultee Basic Trainers before having to cope with the Harvard. 'In at the deep end' was the phrase that came to our minds.

One did not even actually have to fly a Master to be frightened by it. If one was a little exuberant on the priming pump when starting the engine, it would catch fire instead of starting. One then had to keep the starter turning while a hapless airman held his cap over the air intake to starve the flames. If one did get the priming right the propeller would slowly and grindingly rotate, then just when one had decided that it was not going to start, there would be a deafening explosion and one would find oneself experiencing the sort of sensation that could only be replicated by sitting on a washing machine with an unbalanced load in high-speed spin mode.

In the air one did learn to respect the plane's little foibles but it was always ready to trap the unwary into a vicious high-speed stall. One even, eventually, got used to its brick-like glide.

It was said that no one 'failed' a Master course – if you lived, you passed.

The Master has always seemed to typify the sort of mess in which the Air Ministry could find itself embroiled. In the mid-1930s, with new, fast monoplane fighter aircraft in the offing, the need was recognised for a suitable machine for training pilots to fly them. Messrs Miles came up with an aircraft that not only handled like a Spitfire or Hurricane but also almost matched their speed and rate of climb. Moreover it was made of wood so that it did not impinge upon the raw materials and skills required for operational aircraft construction. It had an additional big plus: it used an up-rated version of the Rolls-Royce Kestrel engine, which had been the mainstay of the RAF for years, thus made no demands on the production line for the new Merlin engine which was to be fitted to the new fighters. It was then found that the Kestrel would not be available in up-rated form, which knocked some 40 mph off the speed of the prototype. Still, not to worry, it was still fast and still handled like a Spitfire or a Hurricane.

Things were fine until more Masters were ordered and Rolls Royce said, 'Sorry, squire, didn't anyone tell you? We've stopped the Kestrels, that line is now making Peregrines and they are all wanted for the Whirlwind'. So they had to do a spot of redesign and use Bristol Mercury engines, which had 20 per cent more power and went like a bat out of hell.

Thus, they had the Master Mark II, and everyone was happy until it was found that there were no Mercurys. Panic was averted by installing Pratt & Whitney Wasp Junior engines and calling it the Mark III. This version was a bit down on power compared with the Mark IIs. Then someone unearthed a whole stack of Mercury engines, so the Mark III was abandoned and they went back to the Mark II. It was no wonder, after all that, that the aeroplane was short-tempered.

Most of our aircraft were Mark IIs with the Mercurys, which on take-off gave them a savage tendency to swing to the right. One had to apply full left rudder trim, firmly lock one's leg to hold the rudder bar hard left and hope for the best. The rub was that there were several Mark Is fitted with the Kestrels. These were very similar, except that the propeller went round the other way, demanding full right trim and full right boot. This was, of course, not a problem unless you forgot which variety you were flying!

We had the best instructors, both air and ground. Of the latter the chief navigation instructor was a gifted teacher. He was able to cite for every situation a mnemonic so filthy as to be quite unforgettable.

We were also fortunate to have a renowned and accessible college commandant, Air Commodore Probyn. He made a point of entertaining every one of us to tea in his flat at the top of the college building. Following distinguished service with the RFC on the Western Front he was 'resting' as a coastal reconnaissance pilot at Llangefni (later Mona) on Anglesey when the Armistice was declared in 1918. He celebrated by flying under both Menai bridges (although this feat was eclipsed the next day by someone flying an airship under them!). His tales of Iraq and other exotic postings were a privilege to hear. He was a keen private pilot who flew until he was eighty-seven.

My flying instructor was Sergeant Bowman, a cheerful young Yorkshireman whose skill and patience eventually got me off solo in one of these terrifying aeroplanes. As I recall, I did the deed early one afternoon (we flew in the mornings with ground school in the afternoons and vice versa), and was given the rest of the day off. A rumour went round that there was an Anson (a medium-sized, twin-engined ex-maritime reconnaissance aircraft, by then demoted to a communications role), about to go on a short flight from North Airfield and that there might be a chance of a ride. I rushed over to North Airfield and indeed there was an 'Annie' standing expectantly with the door open and engines running. When I got close I saw that it was full (and I mean full) of men, women, kit and bicycles, so I eased my pace assuming that I was too late. However, despite there apparently being standing room only, enthusiastic gestures urged me aboard. With my white college armband earning me a few 'sirs', space was most deferentially made enabling me to squeeze up to the front, where there was indeed a seat into which I was politely assisted. It was the pilot's seat.

From my brief acquaintance with the Master, the instruments were familiar except that there were two of most of them. What was disconcerting was the wheel and right-hand throttles, whereas I was used to a stick and left-hand throttle. Ordinarily, someone with my limited experience would be required to go through a conversion course before being allowed to fly such an aircraft unsupervised and have to pile up many hours before being allowed to carry passengers. I protested that I had never flown this sort of aeroplane before but was assured that I would soon get the hang of it. Sensing my diffidence someone sitting behind me said that he would work the throttles, which would leave me free to concentrate on the wheel. My objection that I did not know what speeds and settings to use were drowned out by an impatient chorus of 'Why are we waiting?', and inferences that if these people did not reach their destination in time serious repercussions would ensue for all concerned.

I managed to taxi surprisingly well and to position myself at the downwind end of the grass field, turn and call for full power. As the overloaded machine lumbered towards the far hedge the possibility of clearing that hedge seemed alarmingly remote, but when things were just getting into their stride there was an agonised female scream of 'STOP IT!' and both engines simultaneously failed. I managed to locate the brake and bring the whole lot to a halt, much relieved that now I would not be called upon to try to fly this thing. However, it still seemed to leave the matter of apparent attempted rape to be resolved. As the de facto if not the *de jure* captain of the vessel would I be obliged to put the offender in irons?

Actually, the scream was from a WAAF who thought she had left her bicycle behind and the loss of power was the result of someone closing the throttles in response to this emergency.

The girl found that her bicycle had been on board after all, hidden under a pile of kit bags, and so all this taxiing thing had to be gone through again. The second attempt at take-off was easier and entirely successful, but as we climbed away at a speed that was an average of the various opinions expressed, I had to ask where we were going. Everyone shouted a name and there were offers to show me on a map – only we did not have a map.

There seemed to be some consensus that if we kept to the right a bit we would be all right. The undercarriage was hand-cranked but after everyone within reach had got fed up with cranking I decided to let it dangle. We flew over several airfields before we found one with letters on the signals square that someone called out was the right place (I later found that it was Coningsby).

There was no question of using the radio, as no one knew how to work it and anyway I did not have a headphone helmet, so we just pointed towards a runway that some smoke suggested was into wind. Somehow we managed to get the wheels locked down and when someone operated the flaps we went for it. I made a perfect (well, almost perfect) landing that proved not too difficult since the resemblance between an Anson and a trolleybus was really quite close.

Unfortunately, this is when things went pear-shaped. There was a big sign at the control tower saying 'Visiting Aircraft Report Here', so I turned towards it. Sadly the grass, though probably adequate for half a ton of Tiger Moth or even a ton of Master, could not cope with five tons of Anson, so immediately one wheel left the runway it sank. So there we were stuck half on and half off the runway, effectively blocking it, with the tower flashing a red Aldis lamp at us.

My wits-gathering was seriously impeded by the sudden arrival of a score of Lancasters making their wishes to land on that runway clear by buzzing us at nought feet with every visible crew member making vulgar gestures. These aircraft had no bomb doors and in the bomb bays were most odd mountings. They were, of course, 617 Squadron, equipped to carry 'bouncing bombs'; I discovered years later they were relocating while concrete runways were laid at their home base, Scampton.

With the aid of two men, who had ambled out with one shared shovel, my passengers crouched under the drooping wing in the manner of a Roman *testudino*, and managed to lift and walk the aircraft round until the offending wheel was back on the runway. The 617 squadron C/O Wing Commander Holden, was not best pleased with all of this, but fortunately before he could get at me I was whisked away by the quick-thinking WAAF driver of the car, who had pursued us across Lincolnshire carrying the proper pilot.

8

Wings: The Ultimate Bird Puller

WE WERE TAUGHT to fly and maintain aeroplanes, and a host of ancillary skills. We were also taught to be calm under all conditions.

One evening, in the billiards room someone was lining up a difficult screw shot calling for a lot of side, when the door was kicked open by a goose-stepping *Feldwebel* in full Nazi rig, brandishing a pistol and shouting *'Hände hoch'*.

It was by no means immediately apparent that it was in fact a (drunk) gunnery instructor who had borrowed a uniform from the 'know your enemy' display.

The reaction from those present was a concerted and sibilant 'Sssh!', whilst the player at the table, glanced up, gave the intruder a 'looks could kill' stare and re-addressed the cue ball.

The problem of 'games' loomed large, as to play games was a basic requirement anywhere in the service and to excel at games was paramount. Thus, it was unwise to actually play any game in case one's inadequacies were revealed. Obviously, it was best to identify some sport with slightly upper-class connotations, for which there were no facilities readily. Claiming prowess at polo or at real tennis was probably going a bit far and croquet a bit wimpish. However, although courts were available, squash was a safe bet, since as it was played behind closed doors ones shortcomings were not on public display. In fact, it was not really necessary to actually play. I recall two total dunderheads who obtained commissions by regularly jogging past the Commanding Officer's window in the direction of the squash courts, in PT kit with towels round their necks carrying borrowed rackets (uncased, of course, to show that they were not the mere badminton or tennis variety). They would then creep back an hour later in a state of mock exhaustion.

Actually, rugby was the ideal sport. Talking of 'Twickers' always went down well and being a 'rugger bugger' proved you were 'made of the right stuff' and a 'sound team man'. The trouble was that one might actually have to play it and the idea of facing fifteen ugly giants all intent on doing you evil never did appeal. I had played hockey at village level (at least with hockey you had a weapon with which to defend yourself), so to claim prowess at it was not an outright lie. Hockey 'ticked all the boxes'. It was a team game, it had a slightly posh cachet, one could discuss leagues and cups, shields and the like, with little fear of contradiction, and since it was unlikely that a team could be put together, especially as there were no sticks, there was no danger of ever having to play.

When faced with compulsory sport, I always chose cross-country running. Even the slowest could complete the course and be in to bath and tea ahead of the footballers, plus there was often the opportunity for a short cut. One might even be able to thumb a lift and if the worst came to the worst one could always double up with a crippling stitch and be picked up by the ambulance.

Another problem was bicycles, of which there were none on issue. A bicycle was essential and this lack was admirably met by one of the civilian ground-school instructors. He would sell you a bicycle for £4, guaranteeing to buy it back for £3 at the end of one's stay. It was a useful service but finding the initial equivalent of more than eleven days' pay was a strain on one's pocket. Regrettably for such an august institution, bicycle 'borrowing' was endemic. This could be countered by painting your name on it in Air Force yellow paint, so that when abandoned, the machine could be identified and eventually resorted to its owner. However, RAF Cranwell at that time was home to numerous training establishments in addition to the college, so any loss might involve bicyclelessly searching several square miles, so one painted a fictitious rank of sufficient seniority to deter potential pilferers.

Apart from perfecting the actual flying we had all sorts of training and practices. For air-to-ground gunnery we had as an instructor a distinguished veteran who had helped to defend Malta in a Gladiator biplane. We practised using a camera-gun, usually on an isolated house on rising ground, the 'attack' being pressed home until we felt we could have touched the house. Disappointingly, when the films were screened all we saw was a white blob scarcely large enough to recognise as a house – the instructor's footage began with the white blob dead centre of the screen, and finished up with the house filling the screen, with a potted plant clearly visible in a downstairs window. We practised dropping small bombs from extremely low level at a cross on the ground – we usually missed because, I am ashamed to admit, we were more concerned with scaring a couple of Women's Land Army girls who were trying to build a haystack, than we were on hitting the target.

For navigation practice we were chauffeured about in an Anson by a staff pilot. A typical exercise would be to set off in a northerly direction from the college dome having calculated a course and flight time to reach the tower of Goole Town Hall. If one went off track one gave the pilot the appropriate course alterations. Having arrived at the destination he would circle for a few minutes to enable one to calculate a course and time back to Cranwell, based on the observations made on the outward journey. One then crouched down on the floor so that one could not see out of the window, until one announced that time was up and the pilot would invite one to sit up and see that the Cranwell dome was exactly below one. Since this was done in perfect visibility, how much this was due to accuracy and how much to gentle aiming by a kindly pilot one could not tell.

There was some cheating. I was a duffer at Morse and during the final exam I was grateful for the surreptitious assistance of a pupil who had been a Wop/AG (wireless operator/air gunner). On the other hand, during the engines exam, which was a very simple multiple-choice paper, I was seated behind the duffer of the course. He kept turning and demanding my guidance. Fearful that the invigilating officer would hear and disqualify the pair of us I whispered to him to pass his paper back to me. I quickly copied my answers onto it and passed it back. When the results were published he got more marks!

As we progressed there was more and more aerobatics formation flying with constant navigation practice – either pilot navigation in the Masters or more complicated dead reckoning in Ansons – and, of course, IF (Instrument Flying). At EFTS the Turks were trained separately, at Cranwell they were integrated with us, sharing lectures. Although their English was very good, comprehension could be a problem. This was usually solved by Yagiz, their very laid-back spokesman, intervening and getting the lecturer to clarify matters.

On one occasion despite the lecturer reiterating information several times, some Turks seemed unable to fully grasp the point. When the lecturer made to move on, Yagiz said: 'Sir, some Turkish officers do not understand.'

The lecturer's response was regrettably direct: 'I don't care if the whole f***ing Ottoman Empire does not understand.'

We learned later that a full-blown diplomatic incident arose.

There was another diplomatic incident when one night an aircraft being flown by a Turkish trainee was shot down by a German intruder. I believe that the Turkish Government made a big fuss and diplomatic notes flew between Berlin and Ankara. It was a sad happening, but the German pilot seeing

Trolleybus
Copyright Wolverhampton Archives

DH Dragon AJR's first flight, Parc Le Breos, Gower, 1933

Swansea University Air Squadron (AJR extreme right back row), 1941

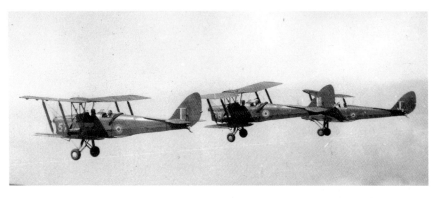

Tiger Moths in formation; 21 Elementary Flying Training School, 1943

Miles Master, the standard RAF advanced trainer. Most were this Mk II version with Bristol Mercury engine, 1943

17 (RAF college) Service Flying Training School, Turkish officers in front, AJR extreme left, 1943

AJR,1944

AJR at 5 GTS Towing Training Flight, 1944

Hotspur II, standard training glider, Glider Pilot Regiment, at 5 Glider Training School, 1944

By kind permission of Museum of Army Flying

AJR in Miles Master II, 1944

AJR in Master II (Tug version), 3 GTS, 1944

Masters in close formation,
1 GTS, 1944

AJR, 1945

Miles Masters being refuelled, 1 GTS, 1945

Pilots relax, 1 GTS, 1945

AJR, 1946

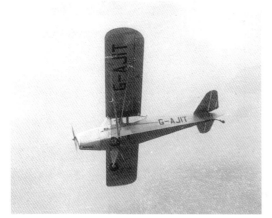

Tiger Moth, RAF Elementary Trainer 1930s-60s, cheap to buy immediately post WW2. Easy to fly, difficult to fly well. Brakeless, taxiing was a 'Black Art'. G-APBI, Swansea, 1959

Auster popular pre-war side-by-side 2-seater, G-AJIT, Swansea

Captain Suzanne Ashton/Hart ATA, David Hitchings (Later a distinguished Chartered Engineer), AJR, with Tiger Moth, Swansea, 1961

Staff Cadet Alan Webber (later a Station Manager, QANTAS Australia) about to fly with AJR in Chipmunk, Filton, 1962

'Selfie', 1962

AJR with Chipmunk, Swansea, 1962

AJR with Chipmunk, Filton, 1964

Chipmunk on approach, Staverton, 1968

AJR with Flt/Lt Hunter, 1972

AJR with Cadets, Filton, 1974

AJR with Flight Mechanics, 1976

AJR's wife (and co-pilot) Delphine with Cessna, 152 a basic 2-seater, G-AZZR, Swansea, 1982

AJR with Fuji, a useful Japanese aerobatic 4-seater, G-BBAPM, Swansea, 1985

AJR with Piper PA28. A 4-seater, which, in its many variants, is the workhorse of private aviation, G-BSXS, Swansea, 1990

AJR with Koliber, a Polish version of the French Ralley 4-seater, a pilot's aeroplane with a 'Military feel, G-CCZI, Swansea, 2006

Many ex-WW1 Avro 504Ks were re-equipped with a more powerful radial engine, and, with the observer's cockpit enlarged to seat 3, gave '5-bob flips' (pleasure rides costing 5 shillings). This example at Brooklands Museum (restored to original RFC specification, including rotary engine) may be one of those which gave AJR his first experinces of 'Warplane' flight. Photo from 2008.

an aircraft bearing RAF roundels being flown over Britain had no means of knowing that this enemy aircraft was being flown by a neutral pilot.

We also shared the flying instruction with the Turks, even at times sharing aircraft, which could be quite exciting. It was usual to carry out IF practice with two pupils sharing an aircraft. They would take turns at lowering their seats and, with their 'head in the shed', fly on instruments, while the other man acted as safety pilot, keeping a look-out to avert collisions (with thousands of aircraft filling the sky this was a necessary precaution). Whoever happened to be in the front seat did the take-off and landing. I recall sitting behind a Turkish guy called Gurol. During approach the perspective of the runway became shorter and shorter, as was normal. However, this time it disappeared from sight because we were below the level of the slightly elevated airfield. At the same time our speed fell below the safe minimum. He was grasping the controls too tightly for me to intervene. I remonstrated, but only after he turned around in his seat and gave me a big grin did he set about rectifying the situation!

On our weekly day off we took the transport into Lincoln, which was in the centre of 5 Group, the core of Bomber Command. Thus the town teemed with off-duty aircrew. It was a sobering experience to mingle with these men who statistically had weeks, days or even, perhaps, only hours to live. To see these heroes laughing and joking, pretending to be just ordinary young men, was an uncomfortable experience. Going into a hotel bar, I saw a row of RAF officers' backs. One turned and I saw a squadron leader's braid on his sleeve. He called to me, 'Hello, young fellow, what are you drinking?'

It was an unusual experience to have a squadron leader address me in such friendly terms. The bar room was dark, he was against the window, so it took me a moment to realise that below his pilot's wings, there was a medal ribbon, not the almost commonplace diagonal blue stripes of a DFC or DFM, but an unusual plain purple one. Then I saw that there was a tiny bronze Maltese cross. It was the Victoria Cross!

I had yet to learn that heroes are not extraordinary people, but just ordinary people who do extraordinary things. I could not speak – I could scarcely move – to my shame I mumbled an apology and fled.

He was S/L J. D. Nettleton, who in April 1942 had led a raid on the MAN works at Augsberg. This had involved flying for 1,000 miles over enemy territory, in daylight at 50 feet. His crippled Lancaster was the only one to return. Nevertheless, it had been the most successful raid of the war to date, delaying the production of U-boat engines for many weeks. I later learned that when I saw him, he had only hours to live.

For real terror we had night flying to come. We had the opportunity to practice in daylight in an aircraft with windows covered in orange sheeting so that the only thing visible was a daytime flare path of powerful sodium lights. When it came to the real thing it took a disgraceful six-plus hours before I was considered fit to fly solo. There were no problems whatsoever on my first solo flight until I had been airborne for about ten seconds – when the engine stopped! We had practised for this: fuel off, switches off, and head towards flat ground. But that was in daylight. At night, with nothing but total darkness ahead, one was in an apparently non-survivable situation. All I could do was to minimise the speed and await the inevitable. When by all reasonable reckoning I had two seconds to live, the engine restarted!

In a state of elation I built up speed, yanked up the flaps (which had been part-down for take-off) and carried on with my circuit overjoyed that after that little lot the rest was going to be a doddle. I was mistaken, since when I groped for the undercarriage lever I realised that I still had the flap lever in my hand, it having presumably broken off when I raised the flaps.

Flapless landings were a routine practice by day but never

at night, since the lights of the Glide Path Indicator (a bit of kit near the runway threshold, essential for even an experienced pilot) would not work for the flatter and faster flapless landing. Moreover, the approach for a flapless landing has to be commenced at a considerable greater distance than that for one with flaps and I was now much too close. Normally, any pilot who found himself out of position for landing did an 'overshoot' and made another circuit. However, with a dodgy engine it did not at the time seem to be a viable option so I had to make use of the Master's near vertical glide by making a power-off landing. This was certainly a first, since such landings were considered too dangerous to practise at night and were never practised flapless even by day.

I have no recollection of the landing, only of coming to rest in the run-off area beyond the end of the flare path. It took the combined efforts of my instructor, Flight Sergeant Bowman, and Flight Lieutenant Banwell, the flight commander, a week to entice me into the night air again.

Almost at the end of the course I did some mutual instrument flying with my pal Bedford, neither of us looking forward to night flying later, particularly as it would entail leaving the circuit and practising steep turns and such seemingly inadvisable manoeuvres.

That night he did his flying first, coming into the crew room with his night flying element of the course completed. I did fifty-five minutes dual with a Flying Officer Watson followed by eighty quite uneventful minutes solo. With that behind me, taxiing in was a joy. I was about to switch off when an instructor sprang onto the wing root and gestured for me to keep the engine running. He then asked about the weather and the fuel state and I told him that both were OK. While he held the rear seat throttle to guard against inadvertent opening, I climbed down to find Bedford, Sergeant Bowman's other pupil, half-crouched in his parachute waiting to take my place. He said something about his hourage being added up wrongly so that he had to do a further trip.

Much relieved, I went back to my room to try and get some sleep for what remained of the night. I remember Cheney in the upper bunk being cross when I woke him by getting into the lower bunk, but not half as cross as he was when we were repeatedly woken by people opening the door and peering into the room.

At breakfast, I was surprised to find so many people staring at me and one or two even touched me before shying away. The explanation was that when I had handed over the aircraft to Bedford, no paperwork had been done, meaning that the aircraft was still booked out to me. So when it fatally crashed it had been assumed that I was the casualty. Bedford had been caught out by a sudden blanket of fog.

Although I was exonerated by virtue of inexperience, I have often thought that I should have recognised the signs of incipient radiation fog and not so glibly said that the weather was all right. I did, and still do, feel a measure of responsibility for his death. I recalled the occasion in the Co-op at Wolverhampton when he had told the girl to put her own name down for the dividend since he would not be able to collect it himself. And, chillingly, the memory of the exact words he had uttered when he had drunkenly attempted to attack me: 'Unless I kill him, he will kill me'.

There was amongst the grief a slightly amusing incident. As was usual, an officer was detailed to attend the funeral. A most unpopular instructor was selected, presumably because the flight commander seized the chance to be shot of him for a couple of days. There was quite an outcry and it was agreed that I should also go.

Since I was not an official representative I did not qualify for a rail warrant, but there was a collection to cover my third-class fare. However, the officer travelled first class, making it clear that an unbridgeable gap in status existed between us. We met up again at Doncaster where we were to spend the night. The officer announced that he would seek the best hotel, inferring that I should find some lesser accommodation. In the end we found ourselves together at a very poor pub, which had just one room free. He indicated that he would take it. I pointed out that I found it first and suggested that he might care to seek a superior premises more appropriate to a holder of the King's Commission. In the end we got some kind of meal, but he declined to share a table with an 'other rank'. However, he was forced to share a double bed! To cap it all we both suffered catastrophic 'dire rear' (as my old gran used to call it) all night. I derived some pleasure when occupying the solitary lavatory to hear him banging on the door, begging me in tones of desperate supplication, to hurry up.

The funeral was moving, the coffin being carried on a hand-bier to a small chapel. The journey back was uneventful, except that at Grantham we missed the last train to Sleaford. Since Grantham was only a little further from Cranwell than Sleaford, we had no hesitation in taking a taxi – bad mistake.

The claim for a refund of taxi fare was turned down, it being pointed out that we should have waited on Grantham Station for the 5.00 am train to Sleaford (in December!) and taken a taxi from there. The taxi from there would only have cost 8/6, so the 16/- we paid could not be refunded. Our suggestion that they pay us the 8/6 was greeted with shock and horror – that would have involved paying us for a taxi ride we did not actually take. I was seriously hacked off when the officer insisted I pay half, since the 8/- was more than a day's pay for me.

Actually, this was my first introduction to the peculiarities of personal transport. The cheapest way of moving people was via a Railway Warrant, yet the rank necessary to authorise the use of such a document was of awesome seniority. More expensive was the mileage allowance for the use of a private vehicle, which could be authorised by an officer of slightly less stratospheric rank. The use of a service vehicle and driver was clearly costly, particularly as a bus or lorry might be used to carry a single individual, but this could be authorised by a relatively junior officer.

The most expensive form of transport was an aeroplane – yet in some circumstances an NCO's stripes conferred the right to authorise travel by air. I recall as a sergeant not finding the mess lunch menu to my liking, so I authorised myself to fly to a neighbouring airfield to eat.

At the end of training, there was a big parade, and an air vice marshal, with great ceremony, pinned a pair of wings to each beating breast. We retired to brace ourselves for the end of course party. Fathers who were serving officers were expected from all over the country. This particularly worried one fellow who feared that dirty songs might be sung, which he feared would upset his extremely straight-laced father. He need not have worried, as his father not only sang, but led the singing. It was an extraordinary party. Squadron leaders made asses of themselves, wing commanders showed an astonishing command of rude songs, with recitations being delivered by men standing on the top of an upright piano.

It was not a mere booze-up. There was a strong educational side. We learned something of the strange customs of the Inuit people via 'Eskimo Nell' (all sixty stanzas). We heard of the versatility of accomplishments achievable by modern young ladies via 'My Girl Salome'; 'The Old Red Flannel Drawers' provided an interesting introduction to the history of costume. To avoid any misunderstanding with the Turks the rivalry between 'Ivan Skavinski Skava' and 'Abdul Abulbul Emir' was not mentioned.

The Turks took no part in this – not so much for cultural reasons, but because they would be continuing on a Spitfire conversion course. Confident that at least the 'singles' men would be flying Spitfires or better in a few weeks, we departed Cranwell's hallowed halls.

9

The Glider Gulag

RAF SHOBDON WAS sited in the remotest recesses of Radnorshire. It was not the least accessible of air bases, that accolade was probably carried by the regrettably named Royal Naval Air Station Twatt (not even the RAF could cope with a name like that), but it was arguably the coldest and most inhospitable. For myself and my four ex 'gentlemen cadet' companions, the descent from the proverbial lap of luxury to a freezing Nissen hut on a bare Welsh hillside was a shock that could have proved fatal. While changing trains at Leominster, enquiries had elicited that the aircraft we were to fly had just one 'sort of round' engine – clearly not Spitfires, they must be Tempests. Sadly, they definitely were not; they were boring old Masters and, the shame of it, towing gliders!

The prospect had little appeal. Firstly, the idea of flying tied ball-and-chain-like to an aircraft twice the size of one's own did not seem a particularly good one. Secondly, such an occupation was scarcely a bird-puller, and in any chat-up situation there would have to be a regrettable degree of exaggeration. However, a squadron leader assured us that it was vital work for which, he inferred, we had been specially selected. Furthermore, he assured us that it was a very temporary appointment and that we would be moving on to more exciting duties very soon.

Anyway, we were there, like it or not, and being RAF Shobdon the emphasis was on the 'not'. Of course, Shobdon is now a rather nice club-flying airfield, but then, as No 5 GTS (Glider Training School), it had much in common with a Stalag. If Cranwell had been a culture shock, this was much more so, only in reverse. The whole shebang was dispersed over several square miles. The NCOs' Nissen huts were heated with small stoves for which fuel was all but unavailable. There was an enormous coal compound, so daring commando-style raids had to be mounted, sometimes even by senior officers, using blankets to overcome the barbed wire. Some people brought in electric fires that overloaded the electricity supply and filled the huts with the acrid smell of burning insulation. Flying kit and even parachutes had to be used as additional bedding. It was preferable to spend the night in an armchair in the Mess, but such was the demand that a chair had to be bagged immediately after tea and sat in all evening.

Bicycles were issued but on arrival one had to trudge the several square miles to get one's 'arrival chit' (yet another chit!) signed by a dozen departments before one could even put one's name down on the bicycle waiting list. We were to discover that before one could escape from the place one had to repeat this trudging to have a 'clearance chit' signed, after one's bicycle had been handed in. There was an internal bus service, but this was reserved for the Station Headquarters staff. I recall seeing the chief instructor, a squadron leader, the second most important man and effectively the deputy station commander, trudging uphill in the pouring rain (everywhere was uphill and it was usually raining) while a bus carrying a few clerks splashed past. Officers did have raincoats, but other ranks had only their groundsheet, which could form an exiguous cape. The use of umbrellas was specifically prohibited.

The quite extraordinary idea of men going to war in gliders dated from May/June 1940 when the Germans overran most of Western Europe in a few days using gliders. The fact that they had bigger (and better) tanks, more aircraft and overwhelming numbers of troops were all discounted. Their success was deemed due to their dastardly secret weapon – gliders. These machines, silent and almost invisible to radar, could land on top of blockhouses whose garrisons' first warning of trouble would be the clatter of grenades down ventilation shafts. Never mind that gliders had, in fact, played a trifling role: the call went out – 'We must have gliders!'

The first was the Hotspur, designed to be released at a great height and, after gliding for many miles, deliver an eight-man team with deadly accuracy. The reality was that they would have to do this by night without hope of an accurate landing but a near certainty of a deadly one. Sensibly, this notion was abandoned, in favour of the idea that fleets of big gliders could deliver a fighting force behind enemy lines. The advantage over landing men by parachute was that ordinary infantry could be used, with only the glider pilots needing to be specially trained.

Thus, the Hotspurs were used to train pilots destined to fly 29-man Horsas, tank-carrying Hamilcars, or the smaller American Hadrians.

The correctness of this philosophy of having larger numbers of bigger gliders was confirmed when the Germans captured Crete with hundreds of gliders, including the *Gigant* that could carry 130 men. What was not realised was that casualties among German glider troops in Crete were so heavy that their High Command resolved never to use them again, and confined their airborne forays to parachutists. Admittedly, parachutists can be picked off by small-arms fire as they descend, but one lucky shot can wipe out a whole glider-load. Besides which, paratroops land exhilarated and ready for action, glider troops are liable to land airsick and disorientated. (Such *Gigants* as survived Crete had six engines stuck onto them in an attempt to use them to supply the German *Afrika Korps*.)

Anyway, we had the Hotspurs, which we were to drag around the sky to enable army corporals, who had learned basic flying skills on Tiger Moths, to be taught the mysteries of motorless flight (as military gliding was officially called). When we had done with them they would go on to Heavy Glider Conversion Units, as company sergeant majors, to train on operational gliders.

In point of fact, there had been a change of plan at the GTSs by the time I got there. Military gliders had two pilots, partly to share the considerable physical effort involved, but chiefly in case one should become incapacitated. Since this incapacity would presumably occur en route as it were, the take-off would have been done so all that the second man would have to do was land. Hence, having plenty of fully trained pilots to man the whole glider fleet, it was decided to make up numbers with second pilots, who would do a shorter course and finish up as staff sergeants, wearing a smaller wings badge than the first pilots.

We were not immediately involved in any flying, but the five of us new arrivals spent the days being intensively instructed in the theory of glider-towing and of being towed. The more we learnt, the more unwise the whole idea seemed. Apparently, if the tug flew at a sensible speed the glider's wings would fall off, so one had to wallow along perilously close to stalling speed. At the same time, one combined high power with low engine revs, so that one proceeded like a car trying to climb a steep hill in top gear, while watching the temperature gauge rise ominously.

Even more challenging than the towing of gliders was the task of ensuring that it would be done at a less Gulag-like location. It was learned that when an intake of tug pilots had been trained, half would be retained at Shobdon and half posted to the other GTSs, which by all accounts were lands of milk and honey. Assuming that Shobdon would keep the best, one officer and one sergeant were obvious choices while the other officer and the other sergeant were definitely not. This left me as the odd one out and I had to make certain that I was lumped with the undesirables and got rid of.

Happily, there was an immediate opportunity to make my (black) mark. Before the days of 'professional' air traffic controllers (and radios that worked), a duty pilot with a Very pistol in one hand and an Aldis lamp in the other occupied the Control Room and endeavoured to keep order. Only the more experienced pilots should do this, but in true Shobdon fashion, I found myself as duty pilot. I was probably the most inexperienced pilot; I had never flown from that particular airfield and had no understanding whatsoever of glider operations. Moreover, it is normal for anyone taking visual control of an airfield to be in the elaborately glassed upper room of the control tower. Here, however, since the Station Commander wanted an office with a nice view, he occupied the tower while the duty pilot managed best he could in a ground floor room whose small windows seriously restricted the view. My view, however, was not so poor that I failed to see a Master doing aerobatics at low level among a welter of tugs, gliders and tugs towing gliders. Unable to make contact with the miscreant, I took his number, logged the matter and rang the Chief Instructor who agreed with me that it was the conduct of a criminal, but since that criminal was the Station Commander there was nothing that could be done about it. Nevertheless, I logged the matter and reported it to Group. My card was marked – but hopefully, so also was the Station Commander's.

RAF Shobdon had (or so it was rumoured) one claim to fame, it was the last RAF unit to use horses. They had been used to retrieve gliders after landing and tow them back to their take-off position. By the time I got there they had been replaced by little tractors of American origin. Being designed for aircraft carrier use, they were (unlike horses) hopeless on airfield grass, the slightest trace of mud leaving them in wheel-spinning immobility.

Some months after my escape from this Gulag, a cross-country formation exercise took my pal Johnny and I close to Shobdon, which we circled discussing on the radio (on their frequency) the parentage, sexual shortcomings and general idiocy of the Station Commander. Within a few minutes we saw an aircraft take off, climb towards us and fly tight alongside us piloted by a clearly apoplectic station commander. When we landed back at our base, there was a 'delegation' awaiting us.

Having taken our numbers it would not have been difficult to find out who we were. What this fool had forgotten was that if you hear a broadcast you have no means of knowing its origin. We admitted hearing the 'deplorable' comments but were unable to suggest where it had came from. However, *we* had taken *his* number, so we were able to file an official complaint that he had endangered us by creating an air miss situation.

Having learnt the theory of the whole glider-towing thing we were bussed off to learn, hands on, how it was all done. Our new base was a tiny unit in the suburbs of Birmingham, a delightful place with just a few buildings, a handful of aircraft but with an alarmingly small patch of grass from which we were to operate.

In theory, this glider-towing lark had seemed most unwise; in practice it was clearly foolhardy, although the gliders were only eight-seat Hotspurs. Trying to take off with one of these holding you back was alarming. Fortunately, there were gaps in the trees around the airfield that were sufficiently well-spaced to fly between in comfort. However, it was not so comfortable for the glider with its six extra feet of wingspan. In the air the maximum towing speed of the glider was only a hair's breadth above the stalling speed of the tug.

Once we had the towing of gliders mastered, we found that we were expected to be able to *fly* the gliders. Now, our conception of gliding was slithering silently and effortlessly through the air. Not so! The take-off was like speeding across a wooden bridge in a train with square wheels. The landing was like a brief bombardment of a barrel factory, whilst the flight was like being marooned in a flimsy outhouse in winter gale. The flight was frightening for two reasons – firstly because one had no confidence whatsoever that one was going to be able to touch down on the tiny bit of grass, and secondly because you were aware that your life was dependent on a bit of kit designed to last one flight only, that had probably already done hundreds.

As for the controls, in a proper aeroplane one called the 'joy stick' the spade grip – in the gliders they were *actual* garden spade handles. The landing-flap lever was a massive wooden inverted A; you grasped one leg and heaved it as hard back as far as you could. This brought the second leg within reach and you then heaved this back. The trouble was that as you let go of the first bit and reached forward to grasp the second bit the whole thing was liable to fly forward. This, apart from stalling the machine, caused the tinplate fittings to slice your sleeve and possibly slit your forearm to the bone as well as tearing your watch off your wrist and flinging it against the windscreen.

Having gone through the training cultivating a reputation for casualness in appearance and general conduct (I once flew in pyjamas and dressing gown), I was, however, judged competent in both towing and gliding. I was confident that on return to Shobdon, I would be got rid of on an ASAP basis.

But no, we all had to go through it all again – by night!

After my experience of my first night solo at Cranwell, I was not hugely enthusiastic, my misgivings not being eased by a tug suffering engine failure on a night take-off, killing the two pilots aboard.

This tragedy had a Shobdon twist. The instructor in the glider, by an incredible feat of airmanship, crash-landed alongside the blazing tug and made a sadly unsuccessful attempt to rescue the two occupants. Instead of being hailed for his heroism, he was placed under arrest and a request was sent to Group for him to be court martialled for 'wilfully endangering an aircraft'. Happily, the request was refused by Group, who awarded him an immediate Air Force Cross (AFC).

Night towing did have one compensation: in the darkness one could not see how close the trees really were. Apart from that, night gliding offered no redeeming features whatsoever, it was truly a 'men from the boys' undertaking. In the quasi-urban location of Wolverhampton and the huge hutted expanse of Cranwell, there was usually enough stray light to at least show which way was up and which was down. At Shobdon, with fields and forests, there was nothing except black in every direction. It was like being shut in the cupboard under the stairs with a sack over one's head. Being towed off and following the tug up to the usual 2,000 feet was not difficult as there was a blue light on the rudder and each wing tip of the tug and provided you kept those three lights in a line you could not go far wrong.

The 'courage to the sticking point' time came when, at 2,000 feet, with the dimly perceived candles that were the flare path on your left, you had to pull the red knob! The irrevocable step taken, a cold feeling crept up your back as the three little blue lights of the tug shrank and vanished and you felt utterly alone. By day, one did not realise how much wind noise there was. By night, the rush of air assumed a banshee quality almost, but not quite, drowning out the creaks and groans indicating that the contrivance in which you were seated was about to fall apart and reminding one that this glider, designed to survive just one flight, had already done many hundreds. Then in a 'bowels to water' moment you realised that the flare path lights had also vanished. You felt that you were the last person alive on the planet.

A quick right-left bank thankfully established that one had drifted over the row of candles that was the flare path. These served to remind one that below was the earth's surface and that one was drifting inexorably towards it and that one had a life expectancy of less than four minutes unless you did something about it. We had done it all before with an instructor, knowing that if we made a pig's ear of it, from behind would come the welcome words, 'I have control'. Now behind was just an empty seat. There was not even a nice big engine to keep you company – just the howls and the creaks.

The big problem was that normally when 'blind flying', that is to say without any external references, you keep your eyes steadfastly fixed on the instrument panel, constantly scanning the six basic flying instruments in turn ready to make instant appropriate corrections. However, with a glider you had to keep looking out of the window to keep those damned flares in view. Having located the flares you refocused on the instruments, only to find that speed, attitude, turn and bank and gyro were all haywire. The only ones you could make any sense of were the altimeter, which was unwinding at an alarming rate, and the rate of climb, that would be showing an inexorable descent. All of which reminded one that the ground, although invisible, was approaching at an alarming rate, that contact was inevitable and that you were solely responsible for the manner in which that contact would occur. Whilst pondering this you generally found that the flares had again disappeared.

Being honest, I suppose the approach and landing were not too taxing, since all you had to do was arrive above two successive flares and follow a laid-down procedure if you were not at the right height at either point. The siting of these lead-in flares was determined by the wind speed and direction and in fact the use of a similar formula relating to height and distance with corrective procedures, would half a century later enable the landing of Space Shuttles.

Having passed all elements, fortunately I succeeded in getting a 'bottom of the class' report that ensured a posting out of this Stalag-like establishment. I was assisted by a fortuitous incident. Tug aircraft, once relieved of their gliders, had to make a dirty dart down to 400 feet to drop the rope in a designated target area. I was terrible at this and on one occasion during training dropped rope across a main road alongside the airfield. Regrettably, it acted as an arrester wire to an approaching coal lorry. It abruptly stopped the lorry but not the coal, which surged forward, overwhelming the cab. Fortunately, the driver and mate were unhurt, as before the vehicle had come to rest, they had leapt out with their hands in the air believing that they were victims of a hijack.

10

Cosy in the Cotswolds

HAPPILY, I FINISHED up in a most delightful place, where I shared a room with a dreadful ginger-haired Londoner (who became my lifelong friend). The room was in a snug wooden hut a few yards from the Sergeants' Mess, which was less than 100 yards from the flight office and crew room. It was called Stoke Orchard, which had a sort of English country garden ring – it was not misnamed.

In my anxiety to ensure that Shobdon would want to pass me on I may have over-egged the pudding, and the reports that preceded me did not impress my new superiors. Therefore, a campaign of character redemption was called for. At the same time it was all a culture shock to be released from the pressures of training and to settle into Stoke's measured pace. The Glider Pilot Regiment was up to strength and we were merely topping up the requirements – relentlessness had been replaced by routine. In addition I now could savour the privileges of Senior NCO rank. Rank also carried responsibilities, as I found out on the first evening I was there.

I decided to acquire some local knowledge by taking the Station bus into Cheltenham. I cannot recall how I spent the evening, but I certainly recall making my way to the car park behind the Town Hall to catch the bus back.

In was dark and in the wartime blackout, dark meant dark. I was accosted by a call of 'sergeant'. I was too new in the rank to respond immediately, but found myself confronted by a policeman with two WAAFs, drunkenly clinging to each arm.

'Two of yours, I think', he said propping them against me. I managed to elicit that they were not two of ours but belonged to an airfield some 20 miles away.

'I don't want them,' I pleaded

'I certainly don't,' said the policeman.

'What shall I do with them?' I was begging by now.

He made a very coarse suggestion *sotto voce* before indicating that it was now my problem and slipping away into the blackout.

In the meantime, the girls, who were just about capable of speech, made it clear that the policeman's suggestion would not necessarily be out of the question, provided that I could deliver them to their quarters at Bibury (wherever that was). Apart from anything else this was logistically impossible, so having happened to notice the police station earlier in the evening, I decided that was the place to seek advice.

Using a sort of 'it takes three to tango' choreography I managed to get us all there. The desk sergeant was helpfulness itself. He offered to accommodate them, and in the morning, when they were 'feeling better', as he tactfully put it, he would send them on their way with no question of any charges being brought. He added apologetically that there would be a fee of 6d, which covered the exclusive use of a cell plus a cup of tea in the morning.

The problem was that they claimed to have no money, offering to be strip-searched to prove it. The desk sergeant sympathetically explained that that would not be necessary as he was prepared to accept their protestations of indigence, but pointed out with regret that exceptions could not be made – unless there was money up front I would have to take my young ladies elsewhere. I suggested that they share a cell, but apparently this would involve sharing a bed, which was NOT the sort of thing encouraged at that particular nick. I asked if there could be a discount if they did not have morning tea, but apparently the 6d was a set charge and foregoing tea would not qualify for a rebate.

Negotiations were interrupted by one girl announcing that she was going to be sick and the other intimating that she was about to wet herself. Once these problems were resolved, I reluctantly handed over 1/- and departed, leaving the Desk Sergeant bemused that someone should defy the usual economic imperative by paying *not* to have nocturnal female companionship.

This piece of quite outstanding gallantry cost me, in addition to the shilling, the last bus and a five-mile walk. This, in pitch dark, in a totally unfamiliar, completely deserted area with (for anti-invasion reasons) no signposts etc, took most of what was left of the night.

A few weeks later, I had a further opportunity to be of service to a pair of distressed females. Cycling along the road I saw two old ladies struggling to jack up the back end of an Austin 7. I offered to help and having raised the appropriate corner, changed the punctured wheel and was about to remount my bike, when one called out, 'Just a moment, young man.'

I turned and waited whilst they earnestly conferred in whispers clearly trying to agree on the size of the tip.

Once they had reached a decision I was called back, quite certain that I was about to receive a florin or even maybe half a crown. Not a bit of it. One said, 'Save us going back, we borrowed the jack from the garage down the road, be a good fellow and return it for us.'

Since she indicated the direction from which I had just come, I was tempted to suggest an alternative destination for the jack. (And the handle!)

Although conveniently laid out and salubriously situated with an adjacent railway station, the grass airfield suffered from a previous use – strip farming! To maximise the growing area of a strip, its occupier would pile it up into a ridge and now, even after several centuries of modern farming, vestiges of the ridges remained and the field had become like a large corrugated-iron sheet. Thus, when the wind direction dictated that operations be across the undulations, landing runs degenerated into a set of see-saw oscillation with the tail wheel crashing down possibly causing serious damage. There were various 'cures' – stick forward, stick right back, brake hard, apply power – but whatever one did not only failed to sort things out but put you into worse trouble.

The pilots, who were almost all non-commissioned, were like sheep and goats of two kinds, tug pilots and glider instructors, each group considering themselves more important than the other. I found my fellow tug pilots very friendly – when one chap landed his aircraft on top of mine, causing no injury but producing an awful lot of firewood, he apologised most courteously.

The 'proper' ground staff, that is the folk who actually looked after the aeroplanes as opposed to the multifarious clerks, drivers, cooks and storekeepers, came in three kinds.

The 'you bend em, we mend em' fitters and riggers were the skilled men in the big Bellman hangers who repaired and did the heavy maintenance of the engines and airframes respectively. Since both tugs and gliders were of wood, the latter were likely to be elderly, moustachioed, have a pencil behind an ear and smell of glue and shavings. We saw little of them and not much more of the electrical, radio and instrument people who lurked in their various sections.

These, plus the parachute, armaments and MT (motor transport) sections, were on the Technical Site. 'Our' ground staff. The flight mechanics engines (FMEs) and flight mechanics airframes (FMAs) were with us out at our flight dispersal, marshalling, refuelling, cleaning and maintaining our tug aircraft. There was a similar set up (without the FMEs and refullers) for the gliders.

Our flight (a unit less than, and usually part of, a squadron) was led by a flight sergeant. Confusingly, any Sergeant with a crown above their three stripes was called a flight sergeant even if he was not in charge of a flight, so by rights ours should have been called a flight-flight sergeant, but to distinguish him from flight sergeants who were not in charge of a flight he was called 'Chiefy'. He was a gem. He treated everyone from the flight commander down as rather recalcitrant children who had to be protected from their own follies. For instance, one morning I hurriedly omitted to make a proper walk round my plane, with the result that I started my engine without wheel-chocks. Since the brakes were inoperative until the engine-driven pump had built up hydraulic pressure, the aircraft ran forward, damaging the tail plane against the 'chore horse' (the battery trolley plugged into an aircraft to supplement the internal electrics in order to power the starter). God bless him, he saved my bacon by immediately preparing a report, 'Tailplane found to have suffered damage overnight. Cause unknown'.

About half of the mechanics on the flight line were WAAFs. These girls looked after us like mother hens. One of them, a short, bouncy little lass of charming naivety, was from one of the Welsh mining valleys, so the 'Taffia' thing kicked in. Before one accepted an aircraft one did a 'walk-round', checking that everything was in order. She never quite trusted me to do this and would supervise me to make sure that I did not miss anything. She would not let me get into the cockpit unaided and strapped me in as if she was taking an infant sibling out in a pushchair. Due to engine oil leaks our windscreens needed frequent cleaning. To ensure that mine was properly polished, she would perch astride the fuselage, her legs sticking out on either side like a Thelwell cartoon of a child on a pony, invariably complaining that she was ruining her matrimonial prospects. I am sure that she had no idea of what she was saying.

When I damaged the tailplane, she threw a wobbly: 'Look what he does if you take your eyes off him for a moment'.

I became quite friendly with her so I am ashamed to say I have forgotten her name. She always called me 'Sarge' and

I never ventured beyond 'Elayseedoubleyou' (LACW, leading aircraftwoman) and to the other girls she was the inevitable 'Taffy'. I can only hope that such a lovely person had a happy life.

As the light evenings lengthened we would occasionally go for strolls. Such excursions were invariably conducted under 'Queensberry Rules – below the belt was a no-go area – but with this good chapel girl, subject to the twin guardians of Valleys virtue, mothers and ministers, a 'no stopping, no touching' regime was strictly enforced. Walks with WAAF mechanics were generally confined to the airfield perimeter track, ensuring that as many as possible of her colleagues could see that she had 'got herself a pilot', and at the same time demonstrate that 'nothing went on'. In addition, going off site meant changing out of 'battledress' into the tunic and skirt of 'Best Blue'. Apart from the fag of changing at the end of a hard day, they felt safer encased in the obstacle to intimacy that the industrial-grade serge battledress offered; it also distinguished them from their skirted inferiors, such as clerks and cooks. In addition, the more timorous type of girl could be reassured that the sack-of-potatoes look of battledress was a sure concupiscence-killer. In addition, an area of the trousers was heavily reinforced producing what is now called I believe, a 'visible pantie line', giving the impression of an undergarment of serious impregnability. The actual lingerie (I was given to understand) was made of stout material in a design we would now call 'Retro'. Someone who had smuggled a WAAF into his quarters once said that as soon as she started to undress it reminded him so much of the time he saw his Gran similarly garbed, that it put him right off – the garments were not known as 'passion killers' for nothing.

Whilst technically not within the station bounds, a green lane afforded a pleasant walk with little risk of censure for wearing working dress. It was free from immolation by American lorries and sufficiently secluded to permit some light canoodling should the strictures be relaxed. In the latter circumstances, if one was wearing one's 'Best Blue', misunderstanding could arise. Non-commissioned men had a pocket in the front of the skirt of their tunics where they carried a small first aid kit known as a field dressing. Thus young ladies tended to repel a close embrace in blushing embarrassment.

This green lane route could give rise to other embarrassments. It passed a sewage treatment works, not in itself a problem since in the absence of soft lights and sweet music the slow, inexorable sweep of the spray arms could induce a relaxed, even compliant ambience. Unfortunately, if the elderly custodian was about he was liable to deliver a forceful lecture about the mischief cause to his mechanism by contraceptives. It is difficult in these days to realise how disconcerting it was to have him call out, 'Hey, you, don't go putting the frenchie down the lav after'. (Particularly if she asked what he meant by a 'frenchie' – back then it was a euphemism – French letter – for a condom.)

In an era when young men were supposed not to know anything about girls being 'unwell', it was even more cringe-making if he took the opportunity to tell the WAAF how just one of her 'women's things' down the toilet could bring his whole plant to a standstill.

The WAAFs lived in quarters, savagely segregated, in a barbed-wired compound. Not only were the penalties exacted on any male entering this territory too terrible to think about, but they were guarded by woman NCOS of Amazonian appearance and Sapphic inclination, prepared to instantly emasculate any male intruder.

Despite such precautions, an NCO returning from a lively evening entered and undressed in what he took to be his own room. Totally unclad he groped for his bed seeking his pyjamas. He located not one bed but a whole row. Realising with horror that he was in a hutful of sleeping WAAFs, he hastily withdrew. In the morning he was unable to find his collar and tie. At breakfast in the mess, a smirking WAAF sergeant pinned a collar and tie to the notice board.

Actually despite the Waffery being encircled by a horde of randy airmen, such extreme measures were probably not needed since WAAFs were in the main looked upon more as family members than as potential bedfellows. There was good sense in this since every woman on the station was in a position to do one harm. One could not risk a 'woman scorned' scenario with the person who had access to the leave roster, worked in the clothing stores or, more seriously, packed your parachute or serviced your aircraft. With thoughts of one's food being spat on or worse, you had to treat cooks and waitresses with equal circumspection, and as for those with access to firearms, the less said the better. At the same time it paid to gently cultivate a WAAF or two for button-sewing and sock-darning purposes. Besides, with WAAFs in Admin able to pick up useful snippets, anyone with a pair of ears within the Waffery was at a considerable, and possibly profitable, advantage.

We senior NCOs had little opportunity to socialise with WAAFs other than those of equal rank, who were few in number, generally much older and mostly strictly married (even so they were still worth cultivating as darners of sock and sewers-on of buttons). There was, of course, the mess staff but apart from the obvious reasons for getting too cosy, a few were a little too robust of speech for some tastes (Hey Sarge! You've had two cups of tea already, you'll be pissing your bed!)

Generally, 'all ranks' dances offered the only opportunity to socialise. Even then the scope was limited since they were under the beady eyes of their officers and senior NCOs, carefully watching for any unexplained disappearances from the hall.

Most of the girls either crowded together in a defensive huddle or danced with each other. Since it was said that girls that went the whole hog (as they used to put it) were shunned by their hut-mates, those outside the gaggles were eagerly hit upon and plied with drinks. Anyone regarding such expenditure as an investment was unlikely to receive any dividend.

It is difficult to blame WAAFs for the occasional scrounge since they did a man's job (frequently better than a man) yet were paid a mere two-thirds of a man's rate. Our flight mechanics might spend a day doing a filthy job in the cold and rain without proper bad-weather clothing, for the price of a lipstick.

Sergeants' Mess dances were likely to be more interesting. Barred to junior ranks, they relied heavily on imported tottie brought in by the busload. Some were demure damsels, severely chaperoned; others, the 'strumpet voluntaries', were the opposite. These latter provided serious opportunities for the carnally ambitious. By common consent, couples seeking closer acquaintance were accorded priority in the use of cubicles in the Gents.

Where there was intimate fraternisation with the civilian population, it was some of the older men who were the most notable culprits. One Station Warrant Officer (SWO – the terrifying man responsible for discipline), a feared and venerable figure, equivalent to an army regimental sergeant major, was seen staggering down a lane in a nearby village with a sack of coal on his back. For the immaculately turned-out SWO, to be carrying anything other than a pace-stick was remarkable; to be carrying a dirty sack was incredible – but coal, that most valuable of commodities, was something else again. The explanation was that a lady and her daughter down the lane often, and reputedly jointly, contributed to the War Effort by providing comforts for the troops. Being respectable women there was no question of money changing hands, but apparently they expected their generosity to be reciprocated with gifts of items on ration or in short supply. Since reputedly a pair of nylon stockings would cover almost any courtesy that a lady could offer a gentleman, what the SWO got for his bag of coal was a matter of much speculation.

Amongst the younger men, the more fastidious type of philanderer sought discreet acquaintance with mature ladies living alone within bicycling range. Allegedly such friendships could prove surprisingly educational.

Not all local fraternisations were of a regrettable nature.

Some could be of general benefit. At one small unit the night-flying roster was not announced until late afternoon, precluding the making of evening social arrangements. It was usually possible to find out the roster during the early afternoon by enquiring at the local Food Office (the government office that dealt with rationing). This was because the sergeant who drew up the list was in the habit of 'lunching' with one of the clerks. This liaison also ensured a supply of the orange-flavoured cod liver oil concoction issued to infants, the orange taste being sufficiently predominant for it to serve as a mixer with gin.

I gradually warmed to my room-mate Johnny, but he was too liable to seek 'modern' musical entertainment (dustbin lids discordantly banged together) so I sometimes went around with a quiet West Country boy named Owens, not always successfully.

We were once accosted in Cheltenham by two American Servicewomen who wanted to know where they could hire horses. Owens used a local riding school so took us there. I, never having been on a horse, hung back, but Owens assured me that there was nothing to it and assisted me onto a docile-looking nag. In the meantime, the American ladies, having leapt aboard, had departed at full gallop like Wild West miscreants fleeing the sheriff. Owens galloped after them but my horse refused to budge, being content chewing grass.

On another occasion, Owens persuaded me to share a boat with him on the Avon at Tewkesbury to row to Bredon where he assured me we could get a pub lunch. It was a scorching day, but by the time we got to Bredon the pub had closed for the afternoon. On the way back we got caught in heavy rain. Owens had the brilliant idea of dragging the boat out of the water, inverting it and sheltering under it. We failed to drag it up the bank and when we pushed it back in the water it swamped. We them found that the riverbank was in fact a levee separating the river from a bog. We had to wade, knee-deep in mud, to reach a road. Actually, things got better from then on, the one bus per week appeared and dropped us off, soaked and dripping at the Queen's Hotel in Cheltenham (then an American Red Cross Hostel), where we spent the rest of the day, naked, sitting on the coal in the boiler room, drying our clothes.

I found it was part of my duties to take a turn as Orderly Sergeant, which meant being responsible, under the Orderly Officer, for security on the camp during the evening and night. Also, it meant accompanying the Orderly Officer to the Airmen's Mess at mealtimes to bang a table and shout, 'Orderly Officer Present – Any Complaints?' (And make a quick exit in case there were any!)

One embarrassment was that as a teenage senior NCO I could stay out all night if I so wished, yet corporals and below, twice my age, had to be in by midnight. However, the service recognised no midnight – one minute before was 23.59 hours, one minute after was 00.01 hours, the witching hour itself was unrecognised by either King's Regulations or Air Ministry Orders.

Anyway, the situation was that the Orderly Sergeant visited the guardroom at 23.59 hours and at 00.01 hours ruled a line under the last entry in the booking in book, the idea being that anyone booking in below the OS's line was AWOL (Absent Without Official Leave), a crime of the foulest nature.

In traditional 'beat the system' manner it was tacitly understood that the Orderly Sergeant would not rule his line until he was on his way to breakfast, and that anyone booking in after midnight would be recorded by the guard corporal as arriving at 23.59. That resulted in at least a full page of 23.59ers, but no one seemed to mind.

The other duty that kept one from one's bed was that of Guard Commander. Although this was largely a ceremonial duty, there being a corporal to actually take care of things, one was expected to be armed, not with the Sten gun issued to us (ammunitionless) for 'personal protection' (this simple sub-machine gun was made cheaply and in very large numbers; it was said to have been the inspiration for Mikhail Kalashnikov's AK47) but a formidable piece of artillery: a 38 calibre Smith and Wesson revolver, which was issued complete with six bullets – yes real bullets. Failure to return all six would involve a court martial so if one was attacked by say a Nazi parachutist, one would have to make a value judgement as to whether to use a bullet or not. Actually a revolver in inexperienced hands would be more useful as a club than a firearm

Since one did not habitually handle a revolver it paid to practice. To do this one retired to one's quarters, adopted a half-crouch with hands dangling, ready to grasp, aim from the hip, said POOF-POOF very rapidly six times whilst fanning the hammer, one then blew across the muzzle and returned the gun to the holster.

Sadly, the holster was not on the thigh in proper gunslinger style but awkwardly situated on a webbing belt. One was issued with a 'Pouch, Ammunition' and a 'Holster, Sidearm', but since they and the belt were made of webbing of the consistency of toughened steel I could never manage to assemble everything. Therefore I put the ammo in one pocket and the gun in the other The result was that extricating a lump of ironmongery with bits sticking out from an overstretched pocket would have robbed an OK Corral shoot-out of any modicum of urgency. Furthermore, one could not actually walk about with the thing in your pocket; thus, lacking a holster, I was forced to carry it in my hand at all times, a tiring as well as menacing business. In addition, if one met an officer and unthinkingly saluted, one was liable to suffer a possibly serious blow to the head.

Despite the fact that the German war effort was bogged down on the Russian steppes, airfield defence was very much a duty we were expected to perform as a sort of Home Guard in blue uniform. Usually, the RAF Regiment furnished Local Defence Advisors, but we were led by a delightful elderly lieutenant colonel of the Home Guard. He had fought in Burma and had been medically discharged from the Glosters. He was supposed to lecture us on tactics but he lectured us on regimental history with a fervour that was Jesuitical. He would parade us, then smartly about turn to display the badge on the back of his hat. I hope the delightful old boy lived to hear of the Imjin River in 1951, when a company of his old regiment held up a Chinese division of 10,000 men for three days.

There were occasional practice invasion warnings during the night when we were supposed to get dressed and rush to our airfield defence positions, but since no one actually got up, these were abandoned. Instead on certain days *all* work would be abandoned, in favour of an official field day. We all had our Sten guns, but there was just one machine gun, which was entrusted to the navigation flight, a delightful trio: a very young and extremely elegant sergeant who lived with his trophy wife in a large mansion a few miles away; an older flight sergeant who was a cheerful barrel of a man, and a New Zealand officer. The officer had been in the New Zealand Army in the Western Desert. Having marched from Egypt right across Cyreniaca in 1940 only to hurriedly retreat to Egypt in 1941, he decided that soldiering was not for him and transferred to the Air Force. This trio had to carry, in addition to their own weapons, a lumpy Vickers gun, its even bulkier and heavier tripod and a massive box of ammunition. To ease this burden, I joined these jolly chaps. However, the officer showed his powers of initiative by stealing a wheelbarrow to carry everything and, not a person to shirk responsibility, insisted on wheeling the barrow himself. Despite protestations that we were a mechanised unit that could rapidly respond to a call to arms, the station commander was not impressed – neither was the colonel.

A more congenial extra duty was visiting some of the many firms and factories engaged in war manufacture. A dozen or so of us would be bussed to one of these enterprises and move amongst the workers telling them what a fine job they were doing (at several times our rate of pay!), and then, having lunched in the canteen, one of us would make a short speech to the assembled workers urging them to keep at it.

The first factory I visited was making aircraft instruments and on the factory floor rows and rows of women in headscarves were operating fly-presses making tiny anonymous components. Spotting at the end of the line a quite stunning blonde, clearly not above sixteen, I ambled over and watched her. She really was a little darling – like a Shirley Temple doll – and was thump, thump, thumping away at her fly-press in a most fetching manner, totally ignoring me.

I have never claimed to be the best-looking guy on the planet but with my Brylcreemed hair and my pilot's wings I was surely worth a glance; however, she continued to rhythmically thump, thump, thump her press as if I were not there.

I ventured to speak. 'What are those things you are making?'

Neither breaking rhythm, nor sparing me a glance, she spoke out of the corner of her mouth, 'F****d if I know.'

Now, for a young man who had never before heard a female use that word, I managed to keep my aplomb remarkably well and continued with my set speech something to the effect that people like her were doing a wonderful job etc, etc.

She momentarily paused her thump-thump-thump to face me squarely and say, 'Why don't you f*** off for f***'s sake, I'm on f***ing piece-work!'

I had been unaware that any female knew that word, let alone used it. I took her advice.

This factory was quite close to our airfield. It had a female hostel, with a barbed-wire perimeter patrolled by large men of unattractive manner, equipped with cudgels. Thus any assignation had to be conducted extra-murally al fresco.

This caused some problems since it bordered the road between the airfield and the pub. Firstly, relieving oneself by the roadside after dark was liable to give rise to girlish screams and angry male protests, usually with an American accent. Secondly, although used contraceptives decorated the hedgerows in profusion, they also carpeted the roadway, making bicycling, and even walking, hazardous.

One of our number, a particularly unpleasant and incompetent officer, claimed that not only had he found a way of penetrating the hostel's defences, but had made acquaintance with a most accommodating lady whose somewhat advanced age and lack of comeliness was more than made up by a wealth of experience and innovation. He regaled us on a daily basis with accounts of her broad and exotic repertoire. We dismissed these as products of a particularly disgusting imagination until, much to our delight, he was whisked away to a 'special' hospital, suffering from a 'mystery illness'.

11

The Itch for Action

IN THE MEANTIME, there was the day job to be done, which involved spells at RAF Northleach, now long subsumed by the Northleach bypass. It was a tiny and informal unit. One hut for officers, one for NCOs and one for airmen. A mess hut trisected into officers, sergeants and other ranks (there were no WAAFs). There were no trainees as they were being bussed in daily from Stoke Orchard by a WAAF driver who spent her day engrossed in a brown-paper covered tome that she never left unattended. Someone who claimed to have achieved an over-the-shoulder glimpse claimed that it was an illustrated sex manual – a rare prize indeed in those days.

My first day there I was Orderly Sergeant and checking through the list of duties found that there was no gate log to check (there wasn't a gate) but I was expected to parade all personnel at sunset to lower the flag, and parade again at 06.00 hours to hoist it. Unfortunately, at sunset all the men were in the Wheatsheaf so I had to strike the colours on my own. I was determined to do the flag-hoisting thing properly, even wondering if a bugler might be available. At 06.00 I found what passed for a parade ground totally deserted so, with the flag under my arm, I strode into the men's hut – everyone was in bed! My shout of the traditional 'rise and shine' was greeted with a shower of boots and invitations to do the anatomically impossible. I decided that this was a place I was going to like.

There was no mains electricity. Power was supplied from a little hut containing a dynamo driven by an ancient oil-engine, lovingly cosseted by an elderly airman. The outfit put-putted merrily all day until 9.55, when there would be a pause in the puts and a momentary dimming of the lights. Immediately, there would be a stampede to press money on the attendant. Failure to do so meant that at 10.00 pm the cadence of the puts would slow, the lights would dim, their filaments would fade into redness and all would be silence and dark. The largesse bought only a quarter of an hour's reprieve, so as long as the various card schools remained active, the exercise had to be repeated at fifteen-minute intervals. The AICEP (airman in charge of electric power) must have been the wealthiest person in the camp.

The NCOs' hut had big walk-in cupboards between the beds, which provided ample space for kit and gave a modicum of privacy. Unfortunately, there was one drawback. Certain people spent their evenings (and their money) on beer, to a somewhat unwise extent, resulting in the need for nocturnal excursions.

The ablution block was some distance off. On wet nights (and dry nights for that matter) relief could be obtained at the hut doorway. With just two actual doorways and almost a score of cupboards with similarly-dimensioned doors confusion could, and did, arise. If the offender chose his own cupboard all well and good, but if it was someone else's, matters could turn ugly.

Actually, the tiny ablution block was remarkable for its graffiti. Nothing crude or offensive, but a series of well executed cartoons parodying camp life. If something funny occurred during an evening, by morning one could be sure of seeing a hilarious illustration. The artist was never identified.

The officer with the mystery 'illness' had returned (presumably cured) with lurid tales of the horrors of the 'special hospital'. Although the son of a manual worker, he was a frightful snob so he was easily persuaded that his recent misfortune was due to associating with a woman from the 'lower classes'. He was constantly boasting of his sexual prowess, so we suggested that the several big houses in the area might provide an opportunity to move up-market. It was not long before he announced that he had become acquainted with a young lady of a compliant nature who lived with her titled aunt in a large Cotswold mansion. The aunt was very possessive and would only let her niece out on Thursday afternoons and Sundays. He could visit her between times, but to avoid disturbing the old lady any assignation had to take place in the generator shed. As the plant being of the latest 'on demand' type, the engine was liable to spring disconcertingly to life if the old aunt switched on a light. It seemed that the young lady had inherited a great deal of money but (allegedly) it was all in trust until she turned twenty-one in a few months. In the meantime, it was almost impossible to persuade the trustees to release even a few measly hundreds, so she often had to borrow from her friends.

Our chap found himself parting with a fiver (best part of a week's pay for a junior officer) with a frequency that would have been alarming had she not shown her gratitude in a tangible manner. He even consulted us as to what he should buy her for her birthday. I regret to say that we suggested jewellery and recommended the best jeweller in Cheltenham. Eventually, we did convince him that the girl's 'aunt' was her employer and that she undoubtedly accepted loans and presents in exchange for favours.

He must have quickly recovered from this setback since he was soon seeking sympathy (without success) for his anxieties following an 'equipment failure' whilst entertaining another lady.

Being high summer there were long evenings to enjoy the beautiful countryside, close to the quite magical valley of the river Windrush. Besides walking and straw-chewing there were country pursuits, such as rabbit-shooting. With Sten guns. Despite the strict embargo on the possession of ammunition, someone always seemed to happen to have a few 9 mm rounds in his pocket. What the local civilians thought of having teenagers wandering their patch with loaded sub-machine guns is not known.

One disadvantage of our Stens was the lack of slings, so one had to carry them in one's hand, making them all too easy to mislay. The loss of a weapon caused wrath from on high, which the offer to pay the alleged cost of 7/6 (37½p) did little to mollify. Fortunately, no one ever hit anything important, since the Sten's notorious inaccuracy was exacerbated by shooting from the hip in best Al Capone style. There was more success with static targets such as the 'square balls'. These were the 2-foot diameter spheres hung on a gallows at the signals square alongside the airfield. One hoist had one red ball indicating 'Normal Airfield Rules Suspended' while the other had two black balls denoting 'Glider Operations in Progress'. Both colours made an equally satisfying 'plop' when pierced by a bullet.

The signals square was a black rectangle that displayed a 'T' showing directions of take-offs and landings, an arrow to show the circuit direction, and other signs giving further information. With radio communication doubtful, before landing one overflew an airfield to check the signals square. At Stoke Orchard I neglected to do this on one occasion and landed in the same direction as I had taken off, unaware that the wind had veered 180 degrees. As a consequence of this, I found myself face to face with a Black Widow just taking off. The Widow, an American night fighter almost the size of a Wellington bomber, was a hefty bit of kit. We managed to pass, whether side-by-side or leapfrog fashion I do not know, since I had my eyes closed. Normally, such an incident would have given rise to all sorts of unpleasantness but it was decided that in this instance no action was necessary since the pilot of the Widow, being American, was obviously in the wrong.

American C47 Dakotas were occasional visitors. They would taxi in and open the door. Two long planks would then appear, down which a Jeep would be driven, carrying a couple of cigar-smoking, lavishly medalled officers, who would scoot away intent on Uncle Sam's business.

A solitary P47 Thunderbolt came in one day. Unfortunately the pilot, who was a very short man, stood on the rudder pedals to try to see where he was going, inadvertently slamming on the toe brakes. The aircraft somersaulted onto its back and was totally wrecked. Fortunately, the diminutive pilot was unhurt.

American artillery-spotting Piper Cubs were with us for a few days. They claimed to be able to 'land on a dime'. Maybe they could but the first one to arrive went through the far hedge.

One aircraft arrived in the hands of an American civilian ferry pilot dressed in a dark blue flying suit, the same colour as RAF working overalls. At lunchtime, when there were dozens of people milling about, he was seen hatless, hands in pockets, leaning against the wall of the Airmen's Mess. For an airman to adopt such a posture was a no-no, as was the wearing of overalls on the Domestic Site. The SWO spotted him from his office window. Said SWO, a man notorious for his lack of stature and sense, appeared on the scene like a turbo-charged jack-in-the-box, his flailing arms twisted to display his cuff-badges to best advantage.

'AirMAAN!' he bellowed, 'Gityerhandsouttayerpockets!'

With his voice rising to a strangulated castrato he added: 'Git them ov'ralls ORF!'

Zoning in on the lounging figure he screamed: 'Wherzye RAT? Stand up strite when ise talking to EWE!' Standing very close he shrieked 'NIME?'

The shoutee seemed to notice the SWO for the first time and looked him up and down.

The SWO, now incandescent, again shrieked 'Eye Sed Watts Yer F***ing NIIME!'

The American straightened up to his considerable height and replied in a deep Dixie drawl: 'Mine's Hank. What's yours, Shorty?'

Amid shouts, applause and catcalls, the SWO scuttled for cover.

It wasn't just discarded rubber goods that brought danger to road users. We were close to the Services of Supply, the US army logistical centre for the build up to D-Day. There were thousands of vehicles, from Jeeps to Sherman tanks, driven by young men unused to driving on the left-hand side of the road, and certainly not used to driving on narrow English roads. In fact, many were unused to driving at all. It was wise when walking or cycling, particularly at night, to seek the sanctuary of the hedge if an approaching vehicle appeared to be American. Sadly, several men and women from our unit were fatally injured while walking or cycling. Happily, not all accidents had a human cost, although the results of some were spectacular. One such example was the remains of a parked car, less than a foot high, with the imprint of a tank track from front to rear.

The plethora of American transport certainly facilitated hitch-hiking. With the usual generosity of their countrymen, any GI driver of one of the ubiquitous 3-ton Chevrolet trucks would slam on his brakes at the slightest gesture. If comfort needed to be sacrificed for speed, a Jeep was flagged. Once aboard such a vehicle, the problem was staying aboard. The driver had a wheel to grasp; the front seat passenger jammed his right foot against the cut-away side and grasped the windscreen pillar, but the poor hitcher in the back had to fend for himself as he was constantly tossed into the air like a Shrove Tuesday pancake.

Difficult as it is now to visualise, the Promenade at Cheltenham, in the evening, would be wall-to-wall with GIs from PFCs (Privates First Class, with one chevron) to 'top kicks' (a sort of super sergeant), with so many stripes that raising their arm, saluting must have been an effort.

Despite the huge numbers, there was a minimum of bad behaviour. The common epithets of 'overpaid, oversexed and over here', or more coarsely, 'if they can't drink it or f*** it they're not interested', were not heard. The average GI in the UK in 1944 was more notable for his naivety and his simple devotion to Uncle Sam and the 'Stars and Bars' than for unruliness.

It was not always the same everywhere. Men of all nationalities had joined up to fight the common enemies, and finding a dearth of any of them in Middle England had to make do with fighting each other. The White Americans fought the black Americans (units were segregated then). English Canadians fought French Canadians. Soldiers fought airmen. It was a sport. I well recall meeting an old school friend who invited me to join him and his friends in 'beating the s**t out of' the Canuck Canadians. It was many years later that I heard of him again – he was by then a Canon and Rural Dean.

No one in or out of the services could have been ignorant of the fact that an invasion of the Continent was imminent. Four of our tug pilots were posted onto Tempests, and we considered them lucky until we later learned that only one of the four survived alive and unmaimed. All the gossip was that every plane would be needed and that we would be towing gliders laden with supplies across the Channel, so that when we were kept awake on the night of 5 June by wave after wave of aircraft, the words of Henry V at Agincourt seemed very apposite:

> – gentlemen in England now a-bed
> Shall think themselves accursed they were not here,
> And hold their manhoods cheap whiles any speaks
> That fought with us upon Saint Crispin's day.

We carried on in this relative backwater, hearing the war through the overlapping of channels and radio talk from aircraft over France. In the comparative peace of an English summer, it was difficult to realise that these were the voices of men in mortal combat and not some BBC drama. American combat troops disappeared, leaving just the convoys of lorries moving southward laden with supplies and lorries returning northwards packed with raggedly weary and frightened

Germans. They had every reason to be frightened since each of these lorries towed a bouncing little trailer, which carried a machine-gun trained on the prisoners.

With news of a million men racing towards the Rhine, came the certainty that not only would we play no significant part in this particular war but neither would most of the glider pilots we were still training. Therefore, we could continue our own little war against our own perceived enemies. These comprised anyone more than, say, a couple of ranks above one's own and of course the ground staff.

Now I do not wish to traduce those excellent men and women (in fact mostly women) who tended to our aeroplanes and us, but the 'administrators' and other 'Town Hall tea boys', Jacks (and Jills) in-office, had one main purpose in life: to make life difficult for flyers. Compared with Shobdon, we were remarkably free of this sort of person. However, a few storekeepers, clerks and other professional obstructionists were around. There were ways to annoy them.

Aircraft were lined up tail-on to the road that led to the administrative area. On the other side of that road was a mainline railway. The idea was to sit in one's aeroplane with the engine 'warming up'. Standing by a wingtip would be one of the female flight mechanics apparently awaiting your signal to remove the chocks. If you chose the time correctly, the adjutant or some other such person would come along the road on a bicycle. They had the sense not to pass behind you but to wait for you to taxi out. When the aircraft failed to move, and with the pilot safely engrossed in some in-cockpit problem, and the machine firmly chocked, they would eventually risk cycling behind the idling aircraft. By a remarkable coincidence just when they were directly behind the aircraft a sudden burst of power would pluck them from their bicycle and send their hat spinning onto the railway line. If one was especially lucky a train would have run over the hat before it could be retrieved. There would inevitably be repercussions, but one could claim quite correctly that one had been intent on the instruments at the time and could not possibly be aware of anyone's presence.

The whole charade was of course controlled by the wingtip WAAF who at the appropriate moment nudged the aileron, so directly the control column reacted, one opened the throttle.

There were other more sedentary amusements, most of which were puerile, the rest idiotic. One little jape was to wait until an obnoxious officer was Orderly Officer, and then to ring in during the early hours and, having announced oneself as 'Group Headquarters', demand that he be awakened. When connected one would enquire if the airfield was on the railway. On being told that it was, one then suggested that it be removed immediately as a train was coming. For some reason this seemed less hilarious in daylight sobriety.

Another prank made use of the availability of a hand-cranked magneto (used for testing ignition insulation). This, wired to the inside of the brass knob of the flight office door, could, with careful choreography, administer a painful electric shock, which would seriously discourage visitors from Station Headquarters.

We felt we were in a strange situation. With the slightly over-optimistic reports from France, there was a feeling that the war, or at least the European war, was as good as won, and unless one's posting came through very soon one would miss it; although the realisation that one was nearing to top of the list brought mixed feelings, since we were learning of deaths and disablements among those who had already been selected.

It seemed the nearest we would get to war were the 'Fanny Barnetts', as the Doodlebugs were called – after the Francis Barnett 2-stroke motorcycles whose noise they resembled. Viewing them as a novelty, rather than a danger, most of us managed to get to London to see them. It was a chilling experience. There were no air-raid sirens since this was one long 24/7 air raid. When one passed overhead all eyes were fixed on it and when the noise ceased everything would stop like a freeze-framed film. Heads would be bowed in silent prayer – a prayer that it would land somewhere else. When there was an explosion it was followed by a black cloud. A few streets away, life was resumed with a smile and a springing step. This was Nimbyism at its most extreme.

12

A New Start

SUMMER STARTED TO take a breath of autumnal chill. My room-mate Johnny and I had by this time regularly cycled to Mrs Maycock's excellent 'Teas with Hovis' establishment at Bushley Green. Mr Maycock had been a tram driver in Birmingham, but when a generous severance offer was made to tram drivers who did not wish to convert to buses, he and his wife bought their tiny Elizabethan timber-and-brick cottage. They augmented their income by selling vegetables, serving meals and letting a room. In addition, Mrs Maycock helped out at the 'big house' when they had guests. In our time she boarded two Land Girls. One was a rather posh 'Daddy runs the War Ag [County War Agricultural Committee] don't you know' type. The other was from a rather more modest urban background. Both were delightful girls and even after a long day in the field would help Mr Maycock in the garden.

Bushley was reached through Tewkesbury, where we always tried to find an excuse to call at the clockmaker's. This elderly man had no clocks to make and few to mend, so had time to talk about the days before the Great War, when he cycled out weekly to each of the grand mansions to wind and adjust the clocks. He told us about one house where he had, of course, to arrive exactly on time to be escorted by a footman to attend to the clocks on the ground floor. He would then hide behind a curtain on the half-landing until the family had passed down to breakfast, after which the valet would escort him to the clocks in his lordship's bed and dressing rooms, then the ladies' maid would take him to her ladyship's rooms, to attend to her clocks.

It was in all honesty embarrassing to be enjoying this almost sybaritic existence while millions were fighting and in many cases dying just across the Channel in France. Our greatest inconvenience was the drawing in of the evenings forcing us, with our lampless bicycles, into conflict with the local constabulary. We continued to listen to radios permanently tuned to AFN (American Forces Network) with its non-stop diet of Sinatra and Glen Miller presented on programmes such as 'GI Supper Club' with its DJ Corporal Johnny Kerr. It never fails to astonish how evocative those tunes still are – Sinatra's 'Nancy with the Laughing Face', Glen Miller's 'Chatanooga Choo Choo' and a dozen others. It is said now that everyone remembers where they were when they heard that Kennedy had been shot. An earlier generation would say they remember where they were on Boxing Day 1944, when the news was released that Glen Miller was missing, presumed dead.

There were other tunes such as 'Honeysuckle Rose', the less ephemeral 'Sentimental Journey' and that king of foot-tappers, 'In the Mood'. There were names to conjure with: Benny Goodman, Count Basie, and Satchmo (Louis Armstrong). I recall a couple of WAAFs being late for duty, their excuse being that Harry James had been on the radio – an excuse that was held to be perfectly adequate.

At the Saturday night dances in the Cheltenham Town Hall, which were packed with blue and khaki, an elegant, white-gowned blonde songstress fronted a serried rank of saxophonists with the brash, in-your-face, 'Bei Mir Bist Du Schön', the seductive 'Besame Mucho', the upbeat 'Hut-Sut Rawlson on the Rillerah', plus the lovely 'Amapola'; lyrics which brought a breath of the exotic to a still blacked-out and beleaguered land.

Even when, before D-Day, the Promenade was wall-to-wall with GIs, the Town Hall was the preserve of RAF and WAAF, who were bussed in from places whose names remain evocative, Bibury, South Cerney, Windrush, Little Rissington; and glider pilots on heavy conversion at Brize Norton, always ready to seek out their old GTS friends and show off their new elevated rank.

Then on Saturday 16 September there was no khaki. We were not to know that our glider pilot friends were readying themselves to depart the next morning for a Dutch town we had never heard of. Nor were we to know that over the next ten days most would be dead, wounded or captured at a place called Arnhem. Nor, on the 26th, would we be aware that the last tired and tattered survivors would be making their escape.

In any case, on that particular Tuesday, I had other matters on my mind.

That afternoon, I was skimming over peaceful rural Worcestershire on a low-level, cross-country exercise followed at a 100 yards interval by a Hotspur glider. The prescribed height was 300' above the ground, but since gaining or losing height when towing was far from straightforward one tended to remain at 300' above the general terrain. This meant that rising ground could bring you close to the vegetation. Near Tenbury Wells, near to the top of the Shelsley Walsh hill-climb course, Tubby Wild's enjoiner that if you have height, and hopefully surplus speed, you can convert into height, you can cope with engine failure. If you have neither, no chance. This was a chilling thought when one is over a forest with nil clearance and, to comply with the glider's limitations, at a speed only a whisker above the stall – particularly if at that instant, the engine stops!

The silence was deafening. One propeller blade remained vertical like an admonishing finger. Then miraculously the forest fell away to reveal a nice big empty field. There was no time or power for such niceties as flaps or wheels so less than five seconds after I had been sitting behind a perfectly functioning engine, I was out of the aircraft and putting distance between it and myself in case of explosion. I completely forgot that in so doing I was running into the path of the landing glider.

Fortunately the pilot was a middle-aged army captain who, after seeing his visible means if support plunging earthwards, had the sense to let go of the tow-rope and the skill to avoid me and land safely.

The next thing I knew, a policemen came leaping across the field, pencil in one hand, notebook in the other. Having ascertained (disappointedly?) that no arrestable offence had been committed, he was happy to be put in charge of my aircraft, now pathetically prostrate on its belly. I left the glider pilot, an army captain, in charge of his glider, which was at the other end of the field. After telling the policeman that he was free to look into my aeroplane, but must not touch anything since demolition charges were installed, I went off in search of a telephone. (As the IFF (Identification Friend from Foe) Radar transponder was secret an explosive charge was installed. The buttons that operated it were alarmingly easy to confuse with the starter primer.)

I followed the policeman's directions to a nearby farm where I made the appropriate phone calls and enjoyed a slap-up high tea (to my shame forgetting the good captain).

When I did return, the policeman had apparently vanished. I found him crouching in a ditch some distance away. As I neared I heard a whirring that explained matters. The bobby must have leant into the cockpit, grasped the cowling and thus inadvertently tripped-in the rotary converter of the electronics supply. The sudden noise must have convinced him that the demolition charges were about to go off.

I had followed correct procedure in phoning the nearest RAF station, which happened to be Shobdon. They neglected to inform my own people, so a general panic ensued when they received neither sight nor news of me. A young engineering officer arrived on a motorbike, which gave rise to some hilarity when he could not park the machine since it kept falling over in the soft ground. The EO examined the engine minutely before delivering his professional opinion which was that it was totally f****d. He then rode off into the sunset like the final scene of a cowboy film. Somewhat later a lorry arrived with a party of men with a tent to mount a guard on the two aircraft.

Eventually, a nice WAAF collected us in a 'Tilly' (a little Bedford Utility truck). Although I might have been in charge of matters in the air, the gallant captain made it clear that he outranked me on the ground, so while I sat on the floor in the back, becoming decidedly chilly, he sat in the front with the fetching young lady and a heater, thus neatly getting his own back for me having left him on watch while I guzzled.

Going through Worcester, I saw street lamps for the first time in five years, the blackout regulations having been relaxed to allow some such lighting.

Back at camp, my entirely fortuitous saving of both aircraft seemed to be considered rather clever and a Mention in Dispatches was spoken of. Since I had just entered the promotion zone for flight sergeant. I said I would rather have my 'Crowns' (flight sergeant badges) instead. In the event I got neither.

Actually I knew of only one sergeant who was promoted after less than a twelvemonth – but then he did stand out from the crowd, albeit for an unusual reason – the blue/grey of his uniform was embellished by brown scorch marks. Allegedly this was the result of a lady's attempt to iron his trousers as a token of appreciation of his overnight exertions!

Shortly after this it became apparent that our tranquil routine was to end. An avalanche of non-commissioned pilots suddenly engulfed us – elderly instructors from EFTSs, gnarled men with WW1 ribbons, one of whom claimed to have flown with the Royal Engineers before the Royal Flying Corps was formed in 1912; men of all shapes and sizes from arcane units. They were worthy and able, every man-Jack of them, but the term 'barrel-scraping' sprang to mind. The reason for this influx was not apparent, although the rumour mill said that a new Glider Training School was to be established.

The trouble was finding accommodation for everyone. By some mischance Johnny and I found ourselves in charge of the NCO pilot's quarters, which at that time were almost fully occupied.

Fortunately most of these new arrivals were married men who had already arranged lodgings for themselves and their wives without waiting for official allowances to come through but in the meantime needed an 'address' on site, since the concept of anyone 'living out without being in receipt of the appropriate allowance' was outside the perception envelope of the powers that be. We were approached by two such men, twins as it happened, to allow them to use our common room as their 'address'. We let them leave kitbags to stake their claim. Soon everyone was piling kitbags almost floor to ceiling making the room virtually unusable. When two unattached men showed up needing actual accommodation, we handed them the key, wished them luck and took up residence in the American Red Cross hotel in Cheltenham. Happily, even after paying for accommodation and rail fares, the modest rents we charged produced a useful profit.

Apparently, during the last days of September our betters calculated that with more than 700 of the Glider Pilot Regiment killed or captured, to meet future requirements the remaining strength of 500 would need to be doubled by the end of March. With training involving twelve weeks at EFTS and twelve weeks at GTS it would be well into March before the first of the new pilots would start to trickle through. Someone had a bright idea. Thanks to the relentless efficiency of the Empire Air Training Scheme there were stacks of newly qualified pilots currently unemployed. Being well versed in the arts of aviation they would not need the EFTS bit but only the twelve weeks at a GTS. This made strategic sense, but would make no sense whatsoever to these poor chaps who had endured years in the system only to find that they would never fly a Spitfire or a Lancaster. The best they could now hope for was a one-way ticket in a winged wooden shed.

The Army also objected, rightly pointing out that soldier-pilots had the infantryman's eye for terrain when selecting a landing place and acted as a fully competent fighting man once on the ground. An RAF man could do neither; but needs must, and RAF men it was to be. The authorities took their socks off and calculated that if the conversion could be done in six weeks then GTS capacity was more than doubled, thus the date and numbers targets could be met. Even so, a new 'super' GTS would be needed.

This was to be a revival of the old No 1 GTS at Croughton, in Northamptonshire, whose southern perimeter was on the Oxfordshire boundary. We learned that it was to be commanded by Wing Commander Kean (Kean by name and keen by nature), a most able officer and one of the UK's pioneers of military gliding. Apparently personnel for this new 'super' gliding school were to be hand-picked and unit commanders were required to nominate their best people for what was going to be a special programme. Most turned out to be outstanding, but a few most certainly did not, suggesting that the opportunity to get rid of a few duffers was deemed too good to be missed. One officer was so stupid that he actually bragged that he had the virtually unheard-of low grade of 'poor', but was slipped onto the list. I was not on the original list so I don't know if I was in the 'too good to part with' category or the 'we can't possibly lumber them with him' (I suspect the latter). I would like to say that I wanted the opportunity to meet a new challenge but in reality it was because Johnny was going too. I wasn't influenced so much by sentiment but by the fact that our recent accommodation dealings showed that our partnership could be profitable.

Fortunately, I was able to swap places with a man who presumably needed 'Johnnies' of a different kind, since he had just struck up acquaintance with a local woman who shared his 'use it or lose it' philosophies.

I recall arriving at Croughton by bus late at night. Johnny

and I somehow, despite the pitch darkness, finessed our way into possession of two well-situated single rooms. In the morning we were interviewed by the Station Commander and the Chief Instructor, who welcomed us tug pilots and glider instructors with courtesy and the bombshell that the ex-12-week course, compressed into six weeks, would in fact have to be done in three weeks! There were protests that it could not be done, but we were told that every twenty-one days there would be a new batch of trainees, by which time the previous course would have to be completed. We were to have no leave or days off. If we wanted time off we would have to make it by completing courses in less than twenty-one days.

On 24 October training began. It had taken probably less than four weeks after the need for a new unit to be recognised for a suitable airfield to be identified and existing users relocated. Hundreds, if not thousands, of items of equipment had been obtained and installed. Maybe a score of departments had to be set up and supplied and several hundreds of men and women, with dozens of skills, had been located and moved in with accommodation, furniture and bedding found. These people had to be trained and familiarised with their duties, and chains of command had to be established.

The term 'hit the ground running' had yet to be coined; a pity, since that was what everyone had to do. The Wingco chose well. The Orderly Room Sergeant was a motherly WAAF flight sergeant of quite outstanding ability and charm while the Station Warrant Officer was a courteous gentleman who contrasted strongly with the strutting buffoons who usually filled that role. Besides people, we needed to have aircraft. Tug aircraft were obtained by demanding a certain percentage from every unit operating Master IIs. It is one thing to ask a unit commander to part with his best people but quite another to persuade a chief engineering officer to part with his best aircraft. Some were brought in by road, with some of these being rejected without even being unloaded from their Queen Mary transporters. Most were flown in, some only to be rejected and flown straight out again. Those that were accepted were converted to towing specification, before immediately going all over the country to collect gliders.

My first task was to fly to Llandow in south Wales with a glider instructor to pick up a glider. Coming back over the Bristol Channel, the glider man saw smoke coming from the underside of my aircraft, which placed him in something of a dilemma. If he said nothing he might well find himself without visible means of support; if he announced that I was on fire, I might well release the tow. Either would result in him finishing up in the water, which, since he happened to be wearing his 'Best Blue', was something he wished to avoid. Therefore, through crackly and distorted radio he introduced a tone of nonchalance into his suggestion that we turn back. Assuming that he had a problem with his glider, I returned to Llandow and the glider man, God bless him, released as soon as he was within gliding distance of the field. He had the courtesy to suggest that I declare an emergency and expedite my landing since I was, as he put it, 'on f******g fire'. I did so and made a dart for the nearest runway threshold quite forgetting the 300 feet of rope with a heavy metal fixing at its end. This latter engaged with, and detached, the roof of the WAAF ablutions before passing between the commanding officer and the commander flying who happened to be having a quiet chat on the perimeter track.

A subsequent visit to Llandow proved just as exciting. On landing a tyre burst. Fortunately I was able to keep the aircraft on the runway and even managed to taxi and park it. I had to hang about for a day and a half until a spare wheel was flown in, but when it did arrive the Llandow mechanics assured me that it was a 'five-minute job' to change the wheel, so directly I saw them positioning the jack under one wing, I went to the control tower to book out. As I stood there drinking a coffee, I watched the men energetically winding the jack. It seemed strange that the aircraft remained resolutely leaning sideways. All was revealed when the head of the jack burst through the top surface of the wing! They had not ensured that the jack was under the jacking strong-point, turning a 'five-minute job' into a five-day job. All I could do was ring up for an aeroplane to come and fetch me.

As I have said, some of the Masters allocated to us were wrecks. I was tasked to fly one to Colerne airfield (halfway between Bath and Chippenham in Wiltshire) for scrapping. The engine worked, sort of, but nothing much else did. Much to the engineering folk's disgust, I insisted that at least the brakes be fixed, again sort of, before I would take it. I arrived at Colerne in fog, which was a bit of a blow as in those days instrument flying practice was rarely enforced. Thanks to the excellent Drem sodium lighting system, I was able to make some kind of a try at getting in, but since my windscreen was obscured by oil from the clapped-out engine, I had to hang out the side to see where I was going. As a result, I had to make several attempts at landing. My difficulties clearly had not gone unnoticed since as I came to rest I saw that I had been pursued along the runway by the ambulance and fire-truck.

Among the assortment of teased-out old cabs were a number readily identifiable, by the corroded state of the aluminium undercarriages, as coming from the seashore location of RAF Montrose. Actually, such corrosion had been the subject of a serious investigation that revealed that corrosion on port side undercarriages was more severe than those on the starboard side. It took the committee months to discover that this was due to the aircrew's pre-flight pee on the portside wheel which was widely believed to bring good luck. This gave rise to the AMO (Air Ministry Order) from on high that 'airmen and airwomen are prohibited from urinating in the vicinity of any aircraft'. The omission of any mention of officers presumably was because in the rarefied ambiance of the Air Ministry, it was imagined that no holder of the King's Commission would indulge in such a disgusting practice.

Back at the newly created No 1 GTS, the proposed airfield

arrangements were 'interesting'. Instead of the usual three tugs and five gliders, the take-off strip was doubled with five tugs and eight gliders on each. In addition, instead of everything ceasing every hour and a half while the tugs were refuelled, freshly fuelled tugs would taxi out to do their test circuit (done before every towing detail), while their predecessors were still doing their final flights. Thus there were times when there might be twenty tugs and a dozen or more gliders on the circuit. Despite (or thanks to) there being no air traffic control, there was never a collision in the air.

The X-factor in all of this was the weather. With its sideways spread, the normal three-runway pattern would have been no good to us, so a wide grass area was required and Croughton had that. However, as it was set up just as the autumnal rains were setting in, the grass soon become mud. At one time this meant running a very restricted programme, with the grass just being used for glider lands with take-offs and tug landings being on a straight piece of perimeter track. No one could have foreseen that the winter snows would be exceptional so that we operated under cloud bases and in visibilities that normally would have kept us on the ground. Hours lost during the day were made up by night. Taking off in a blizzard on instruments was daunting enough but doing so dragging a glider that you knew could not see you was something else. However, despite this, I do not recall one weather-related accident.

Accidents were not necessarily serious. On one occasion a glider with two pilots swung on landing and drifted across the take-off run into the path of a tug towing off a glider. The two trainee glider pilots very wisely jumped out, ran well clear of the take-off path and flung themselves on the ground covering their heads with their arms. Since neither had been properly fastened, their crash helmets bounced away along the grass...

Now see it from the tug pilot's viewpoint. He is committed to the take-off when a glider swerves across his path. He has no chance of avoiding it, his only hope is that in the few yards it takes to reach it, he will have gained enough speed to get airborne and pass over it. He almost makes it, but just fails to clear the raised cockpit canopy of the glider, which one of his wheels hits and smashes. He hears and feels the impact and sees pieces of Perspex scatter, looking back he sees two apparently lifeless bodies prone on the ground and what appear to be their respective heads rolling away. When he eventually managed to bring himself to land, he needed medical attention.

13

Job and Finish

OFFICERS AND MOST senior NCOs had private rooms in huts clustered in living sites around the village, which were all within walking distance of the Domestic Site where there were the messes and the such like. Each living site was put under the supervision of an Officer In Charge, theoretically the most senior rank on the site, but in practice the most gullible, which in the case of No 3 Site was me.

My little empire comprised four huts in line end to end and a fifth at right angles, with an ablution block set at the angle of the 'L'. Each hut had a central corridor with one single and two double rooms on either side. Two huts were occupied by the officers of a small Polish ground-training unit, the other three by NCO pilots. The huts were of an unusual construction with an outer wall of chicken wire sandwiched between oiled paper and an inner skin of cardboard. The floor was wooden and the whole effect was much warmer than that given by the usual concrete floors. However, they still needed heat, which was provided by a stove in each room, plus one in the drying-room, which was part of the ablutions block. This latter was never used since (a) no one could be bothered, (b) there was no coal to spare, and (c) it could not be used as a drying room as it was occupied by my motorbike.

Duties of the Officer i/c Site included responsibility for the fire buckets and, more onerously, for every other item of equipment, such as beds, chairs, wardrobes, dressing tables, washstands, clotheshorses, rugs, mattresses and bolsters. For some reason there was always an inventory shortage of every item except bolsters, of which there was invariably a substantial surplus. Thus, when an inventory was checked or handed over a simple rate of exchange was devised. For example, a mattress equalled two bolsters while a wardrobe might rate ten. The Polish officers' rooms were a godsend since they kept their doors locked and their curtains drawn. Thus, if there was, say, a wardrobe missing one could always state that you 'knew for a fact' that Porucznik (Lieutenant) Blogski had two.

The most highly prized items were the washstands. These comprised an enamelled basin, below which was a bucket to hold the water drained from the basin, and below that was a large metal jug. These tripartite contraptions (called triplanes or triremes according to one's educational background) were carefully designed. The basin just comfortably held the contents of the jug, and the bucket the contents of the basin. The delicate balance of this overflow-prevention regime could be upset by forgetting to empty the bucket, or by employing it as a chamber pot.

A stove heated the jug, and indeed the room, most effectively. Eventually, one typically would spend the first half of the evening in an overcoat lighting and chivvying the fire and the second half with the door and window open, cowering in the opposite corner from the stove, stripped to one's underwear. The fuel was coke, of which there was usually an ample supply, but coke needs coal to ignite it. Pieces of coal used to be called black diamonds, and its value was diamond-like in winter in wind-swept middle England. Unlike, say, Shobdon, where fuel had to be stolen, coal was delivered weekly to each hut, but only 56 lbs – that is 8 lbs per day divided between up to six stoves. In modern terms that was 600 grams – a lump you could put in your pocket. (In fact, some did safeguard their coal reserves in summer by keeping them in their overcoat pockets.) In order to economise on the use of coal one tried to keep the stove lit day and night and, apparently, some would forego leave in order to feed the stove's relentless demands.

All in all the conditions were much better than those at Stoke Orchard and positively luxurious compared with Shobdon. However, there remained one detail that made one's room only marginally below Ritz standards – the light switch. It was situated adjacent to the door, and a bare-foot pad across linoleum was required last thing each night and first thing in the morning. This was particularly onerous in the shared rooms, since there was always dispute as to whose turn it was.

The solution was pure genius. A string was firmly attached to the light switch and led, via two screw eyes, to dangle alongside one's bed. A pull on the string put out the light. The onset of the dark winter mornings spurred the development of the 'Control, Remote, Lighting, Croughton Pattern Mark II'. Like all great inventions, such as the wheel, it was simple. A suitable weight was interposed in the string, some 12 inches from the switch. Thus to switch off the light one pulled the string then slowly released it, allowing the weight to fall, pulling down the light switch. To switch off the light one again pulled the string but released very gently. The mass of the weight was critical – it had to be light enough not to pull down the switch when at rest and heavy enough to do so when allowed to fall. Extensive research and development established that a used bicycle lamp battery was ideal.

The most onerous duty for the Officer i/c Site was the prevention of 'Conduct Unbecoming', which was Air Ministry-speak for the entertaining of ladies in one's quarters. Since apart from the WAAF site, none of the living sites were fenced and gated, this was no easy task – what was one supposed to do, peek through key-holes or flatten one's ear against a partition? Anyway, the penalties were so draconian that a policy of 'what the eye doesn't see' was usually adopted. The ear did occasionally hear, of course, but most noises could be attributed to a play on the wireless.

An acquaintance of mine on another station was unable to feign ignorance since the civilian police had apprehended one of his men for sharing his bed with a lady. Apparently, the young airman, who came from one of the more exotic recesses of the Empire, aware that naughties on RAF premises were a no-no, had carried his bed out onto the road!

The matter of location was widely debated. Some held that the embargo only applied to sleeping quarters, citing the use of lavatories during dances. Therefore, both privacy and warmth could be enjoyed, for instance, late at night in a deserted cookhouse. Others believed that it applied only to premises, so ambulances, and even the more commodious types of aircraft, were sought for assignation purposes. There was a story that the Duty Ambulance failed to respond to an airfield emergency as the WAAF driver and the paramedic were 'studying anatomy' in the back, he mistaking the wail of the emergency hooters for indications that his exertions were being successful.

One reason why WAAFs were not normally involved in such matters was that any girl known to be liberal with her favours was liable to meet opprobrium in the Waffery, hence the randier type of airman was always on the lookout for a WAAF being shunned by her colleagues. However, in general such men, particularly if they had a uniform fetish, had to make do with nurses, members of the WVS (Women's Voluntary Service), lady bus conductors and the like.

Although watches, wallets and other valuables were sacrosanct, cigarettes were so cheap and so plentiful as to be almost common property, so it was by no means unusual for the pockets of unattended clothing to be rifled by those desperate for a smoke. I heard indirectly that late one night (on my site, I regret to say) a returning reveller silently crept into a room adjacent to his own and groped in the gloom for a cigarette. He was disconcerted to discern that the tunic he was searching was of a much darker hue than Air Force blue and all he found in the pockets were a lipstick and a powder compact. Although the tunic probably belonged to a civilian nurse, fearful that he was tampering with the garb of a female member of the constabulary he hastily fled.

Since the carnally-inclined had to rely on imported talent, all station transport was at risk from gallants ensuring that ladies were safely returned to their homes, the Station Commander's car being especially vulnerable. Since it took a certain amount of liquid courage to commit such larceny, crashes were almost inevitable. I recall the start of flying being delayed until the fire engine could be retrieved from a ditch several miles away. For obvious reasons ambulances were popular, but I heard of attempts to use a petrol bowser, a mobile crane and even a council steam roller as makeshift taxis.

On one occasion an airman used the station bus to deposit a young lady on her doorstep. He was sober enough not to crash it but got it wedged trying to turn round in a narrow road. To his horror the warrant officer (WO) from the Motor Transport Section appeared on the scene. Failing to recognise the bus as his own, the WO very kindly extricated the vehicle, gave the man some tips on three-point turns, wished him luck and sent him on his way.

Such buses were used to take personnel into town in the evenings. Obviously, on the return journey there was always the possibility of some drink-induced trouble, so the senior person automatically found himself in charge. I once found myself as a WO i/c Bus when a Welsh sergeant began singing songs whose lyrics the several WAAFs on board had every reason to find offensive. The rules were clear – an officer or an NCO should never approach a person of junior rank 'believed to be intoxicated', but remonstration and apprehension should be delegated to a person of equal rank to the offender. However, there was no other sergeant on board. I was able to solve the problem when he paused for breath by bawling out 'Bread of Heaven' – which he took up and then entertained us to a fine tenor rendition of Welsh hymns. Less lucky, a few days later, was the Transport Officer. Boarding the homebound bus he pronounced the driver too drunk to drive, placed him under arrest in the charge of a pair of airmen, and took the wheel himself. He impaled the vehicle on a bridge parapet, fortunately without any injuries.

There was one way in which the Waffery wire might be penetrated without resorting to tunnelling – it was by joining the Classical Music Society, which met one evening per week in the WAAF Common Room, a delightful chintz-draped hut with real upholstered armchairs, although no sofas or settees, of course. In this voluptuous comfort one listened to gramophone records, to the click of the knitting needles of a grandmotherly sergeant/chaperone. The chairs were disposed around the room, backs to the wall, so that this duenna could ensure that there were two hands on every lap and that her girls maintained decorous postures; presumably she chose the records to ensure that the music was confined to Bach or Mozart with nothing passion-inflaming such as, say, Ravel's 'Bolero'.

To get back to the job in hand. In order to meet the unrelenting 21-day schedule, a large proportion of training had to be done at night. Night towing was not desperately dangerous, but it did tend to concentrate the mind, particularly if you knew the fellows in the glider could not see you, due to cloud or blizzard. They did have a Cable Angle Indicator (angle of dangle) which indicated that they were in the correct tow position when two crossed needles were centred. The dial looked like a hi-tech bit of kit but was in reality a bit of bent wire tied to a bit of string. The string passed through a hole in the windscreen and was tied with a slipknot to the tow rope. If the knot was not at the correct distance along the rope, the instrument gave a false reading and if the knot, designed to slip when the rope was released, was too loose it was blown open and thus there was no reading at all.

There was always the risk of being shot down, either by a German intruder on purpose, or by a British night-fighter by mistake. To deal with either possibility, at Night Flying Briefing we were issued with a Very pistol and four cartridges bearing coloured stripes which denoted the colours of the flares which each cartridge would allegedly discharge. In conditions of great secrecy we were told what colour we should fire off if attacked by a 'friendly' aircraft before midnight and which colours should be used after midnight, to show it that you were 'one of ours'. Similarly, which colours should be used, before and after midnight in case of an enemy attack, in order to fool the assailant into thinking that you were one of his mates. (Bearing in mind, of course, that German midnight might or might not be an hour or two ahead of ours, depending on the vagaries of summer time.)

The Very pistol was firmly secured in a rack so that the flares would be safely discharged down a tube to be projected well clear of the aircraft. Unfortunately the flares were liable to jam in the tube with dire results. Thus the pistol would have to be held out in the slipstream at arm's length.

So there it was, if one found oneself under attack from another aircraft, you reacted as follows:

1. Establish the nationality of your assailant
2. Check the time
3. Extract the cartridges from pockets
4. Attempt to remember appropriate colours
5. Select the appropriate cartridge
6. Disengage (with difficulty pistol from rack
7. Load the pistol
8. Open the canopy
9. Fire the pistol

This assumes that neither the pistol nor a cartridge was dropped into an inaccessible place where they jammed the control rods ... all the while retaining control of the aircraft, in complete darkness, while up to 1600 bullets per second were coming towards you. No wonder the pistol remained in one's crew room locker.

I was attacked on just one occasion when I was returning from a night cross-country exercise. Navigation by night was easy since there were plenty of flashing beacons, so all you had to do was remember what location the code signified, manage a 4-foot-square map within the confines of the cockpit, and read it, assuming the battery in one's torch was not flat. All this had to be accomplished while your aircraft was being pulled every which way as the glider tossed about. I was very bad at Morse code so that was out the window for a start. Where airfields were lit one recognised their shape. Silverstone, with its long narrow outline, was a doddle, and from there you could see Turweston and from Turweston our own flickering goose-neck flare path.

On this occasion I picked up Silverstone, but it promptly switched off its lights. Jammy beggars, I thought, they've finished night flying they will be all in bed by the time I land. I picked up Turweston, which also doused its lights – only to be expected really, since as a satellite of Silverstone they would have finished their programme at the same time. Flying to where Turweston lights had been I picked up Croughton, where the tower was gabbling on about something, but since I knew the circuit was clear I just dived in to drop my rope as soon as the glider let go. On landing I was greeted by an enthusiastic welcoming party.

Apparently, Silverstone and Turweston had turned off their lights because of a German intruder. Fortunately for me, Croughton's gooseneck flares could not be turned off. Apparently, the folk on the ground heard the German shooting at us and were most impressed at my steadiness under fire. Of course, neither I nor the glider pilot had been aware of anything.

Another night flight was memorable since having got rid of the glider I was feeling particularly pleased with life as I dived down to 300 feet to drop the rope. Normally, one immediately regained the 1000 feet circuit height, but this time it occurred to me that I could save time and effort by remaining at 300 feet. In fact, I reasoned that with the highest obstacle anywhere near the field being the 50-foot radio mast, 100 feet was a perfectly safe altitude, and to prove my point dropped down to that height. The chap in the tower made a bit of a fuss over the radio, which proved how little he knew about it. I made a beautiful touch-down, but on my landing run I saw something most puzzling. The flares on the left were going backwards whilst those on the right were going forwards. Now, with the engine in the way you could not see ahead, so when landing you tended only to look to the left, so in all honesty I could only assume that the flares on the right usually went back as well but on this occasion this did not appear to be the case. I thought it a bit odd that the left side of the aircraft was going forwards while the right side was going backwards. Eventually all the flares stopped moving but with such a strange phenomenon going on I just dared not taxi back, so I switched everything off, climbed out, shouldered my parachute and set out to walk to dispersal. The trouble was, whatever strange forces had affected the lights seemed to have spread to my legs, so I laid down on the grass and, using my parachute as a pillow, went to sleep.

Now look at it as they would have seen it from the control tower. An aircraft did a circuit virtually at ground level. When it landed they saw from its lights that it spun around and around in a tight circle. This was followed by dead silence and the lights vanished.

Very properly the airfield was declared closed and the ambulance, fire engine, Coles crane and more or less every available vehicle was dispatched to investigate. By the greatest good fortune no one ran over me. The explanation was that there was a hydraulic pressure gauge in the cockpit and the new, 'improved' fluid whose pressure it was measuring was leaking a highly intoxicating vapour into the cockpit, thus rendering the pilot insensible. Fortunately, in those days all flying in the circuit was done with the canopy open, thus I had remained conscious but in a seriously drunken condition.

14

All Right for Some

WHENEVER THE WEATHER really was too bad for flying, we were put in the hands of a quite revoltingly fit young woman corporal PTI. I'm not sure about the instruction or the training, but she could certainly get physical, although perhaps not in the way some of us might have preferred. Hyperactive, she leapt about like a human pogo stick, demanding that we touched toes, sprang in the air and otherwise uselessly expended energy; whilst exhorting us to eschew drinking, smoking, and 'bad habits'. She used to cause excitement by nonchalantly shedding her trousers and donning shorts in mid lecture affording an inflaming glimpse of Knickers, Cotton, Blue, Airwomen for the use of, Pairs, 1 – the sole opportunity most of us had to see such a garment. However, this lively and uninhibited girl revealed herself as pure evil with her favourite activity – indoor hockey. An indeterminate number of players, armed with inverted walking sticks, attempted to score goals by causing a heavy wooden puck to make contact with marked sections of opposite end walls of the gym. Goals were far outnumbered by injuries. Opponents' sticks could hurt, a flying puck could maim, but contact with a projecting pilaster of the bare-brick gym wall could be a stretcher case. As I recall, the winner was the team with the most players left standing. Not that she was indifferent to injuries; she was most worried by them – lest the blood stained her polished floor!

Every course was completed within the allotted twenty-one

days (one, as I recall, was done in eleven), but I fear the press-on, gung-ho attitude left some of the pilots under-trained. Plus, having two non-soldiers on board meant that on landing not only was each glider-load effectively two men short, but they had a couple of non-combatants to look after. In addition, a soldier choosing a landing place would consider its defensibility in a way that a non-soldier could not.

The fact that so many aircraft could put in so many hours was due to the devotion of the flight ground crew, who were nearly all WAAF. Young women, who maybe had never previously handled any machine more complex than a mangle or a mincer, kept us fuelled and flying in rain and snow, with the winter of 1944 providing plenty of both. Even worse than handling freezing cold (or burning hot) metal with numb fingers was the run-up. In order to test the engine to maximum power it was necessary to have two people lying across the tail to prevent the aircraft tipping onto it nose. To endure almost a thousand horsepower's worth of freezing gale with only cotton overalls for protection was considered so taxing that WAAFs were prohibited from doing it. However, when an engine's rough running suggested that a full power check would be called for, the few men invariably seemed to vanish, so to keep the aircraft going these girls would volunteer to do it no matter how harsh the conditions. There was no issue of proper waterproof or cold weather clothing, and clothes rationing meant that there was no question of them buying their own.

They (and we) were fortunate to have a most exceptional flight sergeant in charge of the flight mechanics – Chiefy Robinson. How Robbie coped with the demands of the pilots and management, shortages of materials, equipment, personnel and time, coped with tantrums and sometimes hysterics, with such calm equanimity, I shall never know. An indication of the regard in which he was held was shown shortly following VE Day. A number of flights had been arranged to see the bombed cities of Germany. Our flight received one ticket with the suggestion that it be the subject of an all-ranks raffle. Every officer, NCO, airman and airwoman on the flight unanimously agreed that no raffle be held but that the ticket be given to Robbie.

The Allied advance having captured the launch sites for the V1s, a new danger came to London – the V2 rockets. There was no putter-putter, no anxious wait, nothing. The first thing you heard was the bang, and if you heard the bang you knew it had missed you. The noise was quite unique and closely following the detonation was the second bang, which was almost as loud. This, in its turn, was followed by the whistling sound of something departing at high speed. This gave rise to the myth that the thing, having used up its explosive demolishing half a street, had gone straight back to Germany for a 'refill'. The facts, of course, were that the second explosion was the 'sonic boom' and the whistle was merely the noise of its approach, which, being at around three times the speed of sound, was not only raised several octaves by the Doppler effect but was heard after it had arrived. The final milliseconds before it struck were heard first, and the more distant sounds were heard later, with the first whispers of its approach being heard last. With macabre curiosity, this was something we all wanted to hear so London was the destination of choice when we had time off.

We were detached onlookers as the great events in Europe reached their inevitable conclusion, with just a taste of vicarious involvement as our reluctant trainees took their gliders across the Rhine

8 May 1945 came and went, but no serviceman's joy at VE Day could be entirely unconfined. Admittedly, we weren't going to be bombed and no one was going to shoot at us, but there was still Japan. The older men, who had endured battle and hardship on three continents for more than five years, were being released, while the younger men, who up to then had seen little (or in my case, nothing whatsoever) of combat would be sent out to the Far East. In fact, as soon as Generals Montgomery and Von Runstead had re-pocketed their respective

pens on Lüneburg Heath, the Navy was trying to bamboozle us pilots into changing uniforms and confronting the Kamikazis from the decks of tiny carriers that were virtually merchant ships with the funnels cut off.

I would like to be able to say that there was a stampede to strike our blow for King and Country, but the 'never volunteer' philosophy was by now too deeply entrenched for us to do anything but sit and wait to be put on an Orientally-orientated boat for a war that was expected to be ended (and hopefully won) by the end of 1947.

Although it appeared that large-scale glider operations would not be appropriate in the Far East, we continued to train army corporals, albeit at a less frenetic pace. Indeed, apart from the fact that postings to less congenial tasks loomed large in our thoughts, life was largely unaltered. Blackout regulations, which had been eased for some months, were entirely abolished and we were now free of intruders trying to shoot us down. Generally, wartime shortages continued, and food rationing became even more stringent. The one great life-changing moment was the lifting of the ban on private motoring. Petrol could still only be bought against coupons, which had for almost four years only been issued to 'essential' users; however, now such coupons were available to any owner of a car or motorcycle.

Immediately, there was a stampede to get mobile. Everyone who could afford it, and undoubtedly some who could not, bought themselves a set of wheels. I opted for a motorcycle, a massive 600 cc Model 19 Norton, for which I paid £28. My father was appalled by such profligacy, but this sum did include being taught to ride it. The tuition consisted of pointing out which lever did what. I was never shown how to use the kick-start, so I always had to park at the top of a hill. This in due course gave way to a car, a 1932 Morris Minor which cost a dizzy £75, almost three-quarters of its price new. Most aspired to something sportier, an MG, a Wolseley Hornet or an Aero Minx. With no cars having been built for the civilian market, even these tired old bangers changed hands at increasingly silly prices, provided that the tyres were good ('good' meant that little or no canvas was showing). Car tyres were quite unobtainable. Small cars could manage with motorcycle tyres, which were readily obtainable; otherwise drivers had to depend on stolen spare wheels, the theft of which became a major industry. Running costs were trifling by modern standards, a year's insurance on a small car or a big motorcycle was less than £4, tax on an 8 hp car was £6 and on even the largest motorcycle under £4. Petrol in today's money worked out at the equivalent of 2p per litre. Some of these rust-buckets used a lot of oil, which also at around 2p per litre could mount up. At least one comic Casanova wrecked a perfectly good car, specially purchased as a bird-puller, by using stolen aviation oil.

Speaking of which, a senior officer totalled his Austin Seven quite spectacularly. Finding a pub in Brackley closed because it had run out of beer, he smashed his way in by ram-raiding the front door. Unfortunately, the car became wedged in the passage and being unable to open the door the driver remained trapped until the Fire Brigade sorted things out.

While behaviour of this sort was rare, such things as a lack of brakes, lights and silencers brought many clashes with the constabulary. However, as far as I am aware, I was the only person in my circle to be actually locked up. I had at the time a Morgan three-wheeler – not one of the prized aero models with a massive engine in front and massive exhausts on the outside, but a very sober-sided four-seater family runabout. Restored, it would be worth five figures today, but I was well content to buy it for £12 and to sell it for £30. As the law required it had two braking systems, but both were on the back wheel (the two band-brakes and two chains so impeded rear-wheel removal that a puncture repair took four hours), so in order to achieve some sort of skid-free stop I carried two 10-gallon drums of water on the back seat. Among its many faults was (like the Norton) great difficulty in starting, so it also had to be parked on a hill. Since the handbrake had no ratchet, one chocked the offside front wheel with a brick. One moved off by juggling the wheel until the chocked wheel edged clear of the brick, then as the vehicle rolled forward, one reached down and recovered the brick.

Going away by train one weekend, I left it at the top of Brackley High Street. When I returned on Sunday evening I was seized by two burly policemen, frog-marched to the nick and cast into a cell. Apparently, seeing the car with two drums, containing what they assumed was petrol, on the back seat, they had maintained a stakeout since the Friday evening. Thus I was arrested as a black marketeer. To emphasise the gravity of the offence a Chief Inspector in full rig read me my rights. I pointed out that without even a hood for concealment (on a wet and windy day the canvas hood had become detached from the windscreen cant-rail, had reared up like a windjammer's mainsail, ripped itself clear and soared away to engulf a closely following car), one would be more likely (at that time) to leave the royal crown, orb and sceptre unattended on the back seat of an open car than petrol; also, while thinking of things royal, I suggested that the monarch would be most displeased that a person whose warrant he held was being prevented from going about said sovereign's business. I offered to demonstrate that it was water not petrol, but he replied that only the County Analyst could adjudicate upon such a matter. I eventually persuaded him to have a small quantity of fluid spilled in the middle of the police station yard. While he and his constables watched from a safe distance. I threw burning matches into the puddle. It was only after I had repeated the performance with the contents of the second drum, did the CI admit the possibility that it was not petrol. After numerous fingers had been dipped in the water, smelled and licked, it was admitted that it might not be petrol after all and I was released with an admonishment not to do it again.

The police were justified in being vigilant since there was a flourishing black market in petrol, or at least in stolen or forged coupons, which were changing hands at four or five times the price of the fuel they represented. There was obviously a strong temptation to steal petrol, but the penalties were draconian. At an army unit just down the road a senior sergeant of hitherto unblemished record got four months' detention for being found in possession of a lemonade bottle half-full of petrol.

There were two avenues by which the basic allocation of petrol coupons could be augmented. One was by persuading the young female Assistant Adjutant that the journey you were making was an 'essential' duty run and that one's motorcycle only did 20 mpg. Neither task was easy. It was paradoxical that the service was so parsimonious in parting with petrol coupons to use for petrol in your own vehicle, which you paid for, yet was quite willing to let you use oodles of it in an aeroplane on the slightest of pretexts – flying someone home on leave not only became a 'training exercise', but could also earn you money.

The other route to fuel augmentation was to buy a wrecked motorcycle, insure it and tax it for a quarter and claim a three-month book of coupons. You then cancelled the insurance and surrendered the tax disc to obtain a two-month refund. You could do the same thing three months later. Since no MOT was required, the most the insurance company would demand would be a form certifying that the machine was in a satisfactory condition (which from your point of view it was). It was not necessary to actually *possess* the machine as long as you had its logbook.

It was rumoured that aviation fuel was 'too strong' for a road vehicle, hence the idea that it could be used mixed with paraffin. True or not, I do not know, but several cars and motorcycles spluttered around emitting noxious smoke smelling like Primus stoves. I had too much respect for my car and too much fear of getting caught to steal aircraft fuel.

There was also a rumour that despite the reduced activity post-VE Day, aviation petrol was being delivered at the same rate as was needed during the frenetic times, and since no good supply officer ever refused anything, our storage tanks were in danger of overflowing. Thus, there was a feeling that it would be churlish not to help out by consuming this embarrassing surplus.

I kept well clear myself, but one night I had proof that some were being more 'helpful'. When returning to dispersal, one was dependent on the marshaller with light-batons to guide you clear of obstructions such as starter trolleys, oil carts and indeed unlighted aircraft. This time, despite blipping the throttle to attract attention, no batons appeared. Therefore, I put on my landing lights and veered the aircraft to sweep the dispersal area. This revealed that the marshaller was busy marshalling a line of cars queuing up for the petrol Bowser, while other ground-crew members frantically gestured me to put the lights out.

Never mind the breakdowns (I once spent eight hours at the roadside with a sick motorcycle, and once spent the night walking round Swindon waiting for dawn since my lights had failed), or the punctures, or having to put pieces of old shoes inside a tyre when the canvas had worn through, exposing the inner-tube; having one's own transport opened up new horizons. I could go into town independent of buses, go for a meal, visit friends in college and go to the theatre at Oxford. Later, there was a quite extraordinary bonus. A colleague had a double ticket to a cocktail party near Bletchley and he said that I could accompany him if I gave him a lift on my 1922 belt-drive EW Douglas Motorcycle. A rolled-up sheet converted the carrier into a makeshift pillion. We arrived at a rather swish country house, in front of which were a number of staff cars and limousines with waiting drivers. The whole place was stiff with Military Police, one of whom insisted on parking my ancient motorcycle. Inside was a crush of senior Army officers of singularly unmilitary appearance, professorial-looking men, and some women of most intimidating aspect. As an NCO, it was an odd experience having an elderly lieutenant colonel introduced as 'Bunty' and being assured that he was a 'Dear

Boy'. Having accepted a drink or two we needed the Gents – we were escorted there by an (armed) MP who closely supervised our actions. Enquires as to the occupation of fellow guests were met with assurances that they were part of the BBC and it was all rather boring. It was decades later that I realised we had been at Bletchley Park – although the war with Germany was over, I am quite sure that they were then intent on the USSR.

The greatest blessing of having transport was (petrol permitting) its replacement of train travel. It is difficult to describe the full horror of train travel, particularly on main lines at night. Breakdowns, air raids and trains being shunted out of the way of urgent military traffic caused interminable delays. At junctions connections were missed and, anyway, one could never find the correct platform. Worst of all was the overcrowding. On the main lines a seat was a rare luxury and even space to stand was at a premium. I recall spending several hours jammed in the concertina between carriages, much of the time straddling the actual connection and thinking that if the coupling failed I would be in serious bother. In those days carriages were split into compartments connected by a side corridor. I recall once buying a first-class ticket in the hope of getting a seat. I was fortunate to get one of the six seats but when the train pulled out of Paddington, in addition to the seated passengers there was one lying on each of the two luggage racks and nine standing. The corridors were always packed. At one time trying to board a train at Swindon, I attempted to open a door and was brusquely told by an army officer that there was no room. I nevertheless opened the door and the poor fellow fell out on top of me. The crush inside was so great that he failed to get back in and was left with me on the platform as the train pulled out leaving us facing a night trying to sleep on a luggage-trolley. He was really most upset.

At stations such as Swindon or Reading the trains were often so long that they had to make two stops to allow everyone to reach the platform. Received wisdom was that the back half was less crowded so one tended to wait for the second pull-up before attempting to board. The trouble was that sometimes there was no second stop. It was a horrible moment as one realised that the train, which you assumed was just going to crawl a few carriage-lengths, was gathering speed and that you might be facing a night lying on a luggage trolley

An additional problem on long journeys was the difficulty of reaching the toilet. It was worth trying, even though it would almost certainly be permanently occupied by someone determined to get a seat of some kind, or possibly by a number of people dodging the ticket collector. Even with a seat, travelling, particularly overnight, was not pleasant. The person sitting next to you would invariably fall asleep leaning across you and snore revoltingly. The discovery that the most charming young lady could sound like a shed-load of pigs must have put many a young man off matrimony.

Then there was the fog of cigarette smoke and the smell of wet greatcoats. I'm sure the odour of saturated khaki breached the Geneva Convention. Added to this was the inevitable consequence of troops deprived of proper bathing facilities. In addition, with so many people in close juxtaposition anyone with digestive problems did not need to suffer in silence as it were, since there was little risk of the culprit being named and shamed. After an hour or two, even if no hapless chap unable to reach the lavatory had done the inevitable, one could imagine that one was sharing a skunk's nest in a pigsty.

Despite close male-female intimacy and extremely dim lighting, a strict code of decorum was observed. Occasionally, there were disputes as to whether a contact was accidental or deliberate, but these were invariably settled without rancour.

15

The Law and the Profits (And Peace)

EVEN MORE HEINOUS than the theft of petrol was low flying. Before modern radar developments forced military pilots to practice ground-hugging tactics over long distances, low-flying practice was confined to small, designated areas. We had to give the glider pilots experience of being towed at low level, but even this was at a 300-foot minimum. It was not our fault that a famous and fashionable pack hunted in our low-flying area; nor was happening to stray below 300 feet necessarily anything but a trifling error of judgement. Similarly, since many hunting folk had army backgrounds, telephoned allegations of excessively low altitudes could be dismissed as intra-service jealousy, and reports of horses bolting and riders being thrown were clear admissions of an inability to control their mounts.

Deliberate 'beat-ups' were severely dealt with – loss of rank and a sojourn in a military prison followed by a dishonourable discharge and a transfer to the infantry was a standard penalty.

Yet the worst piece of low flying I have heard of went unpunished. The culprit was one of our tug pilots. He was a married man with a wife whose job forced her to live some 60 miles away. Like any good husband he visited her whenever he could and in due course his solicitous visits proved fruitful and she was safely delivered of a son. Immediately he had news of this he took a Master on an unauthorised flight. On his return he was whisked away under close arrest. He did technically steal an aeroplane, but he brought it back undamaged, so there seemed to have been an over-reaction. We were soon disabused of that notion, learning that he had located the hospital where his wife was; finding that it was surrounded by treeless grounds he had repeatedly circled the building at almost ground level in the apparent hope that his wife would realise it was him and hold up the baby to a window for him to see.

We forgot about it except to speculate on the length of his sentence. Then after about three weeks he just showed up and resumed his duties. According to rumour, when the charges were read out at his trial, a Member of the Court exclaimed 'The man must be mad'. His defending officer successfully claimed that his client, having been declared mad by a Member of the Court, was unfit to stand trial. Accordingly, he was delivered to a secure psychiatric unit. There, tests were run and he was adjudged to be totally sane and so was discharged. Apparently the original 'unfit to plead' thing still stood, so he could not be tried for any offence.

The Air Force legal system was a truly peculiar mechanism. At one base where I was stationed we had a warrant officer who had been in charge of a tiny radio station in a remote corner of the globe. In order to boost morale he arranged for a lorry to bring in young women from the nearby town to entertain his men. The story, as we heard it, was that to conserve petrol he allowed some of the women to take up residence. Unfortunately, there were insufficient men in the unit to keep the women in 'full employment' so he allowed them to extend their courtesies to other servicemen and even the indigenous population. A royalty system produced an income stream that built up a welfare fund that could be used for the benefit of his personnel.

The authorities found out and a court martial convened. However, his defending officer discovered that the charges had been so badly framed that they failed to uncover any activity that was outside the discretion of a commanding officer, and since his client *was* a de facto commanding officer, he had, therefore, committed no crime.

I was only once involved in the legal system. An Irish airman had apparently joined up to fight. Since there was no one left to fight, he had assumed that his services were no longer required and hence had not returned from leave. Accordingly, a two-man Court of Enquiry, of which I was the junior member, was convened to take sworn evidence on the facts leading up to this apparent desertion, so that should the absentee be apprehended in the distant future, something on which to base charges would be available.

We were equipped with a room, a manual about the Procedures for the Convening and Conducting of Courts of Enquiry, a WAAF clerk, a Bible, three chairs and a table plus, of course, the appropriate forms. The absence of any chair for a witness was a deliberate omission to emphasise the majesty of the court.

The Presiding Officer, a rather bewildered flight lieutenant, read out for my benefit and that of the WAAF and the otherwise empty room, a proclamation something to the effect that by virtue of the authority conferred upon him by His Gracious Majesty King George the Sixth, he had the power to call upon such persons as might be deemed appropriate to give evidence on oath and to seize and safeguard any exhibit pertaining to the matter before this court – that is the alleged unauthorised absence of Aircraftman Second Class number xxxxx, Patrick O'Something. He then rapped on the table and announced that the court was in session,

The WAAF was the first to break the silence by pointing out that the YMCA van was in the area and suggesting that if she were to be given funds she would fetch us tea plus, if required, a Parkin or an Eccles.

As regards the sworn evidence, there was plenty of evidence of swearing but little else. We had a number of men up before us who gave accounts of the absentee's expressions of intention to desert, these accounts varying only in the forcefulness of their adjectival embellishment. All this was dutifully recorded by the young WAAF, who had to be assisted with the spelling of the more extreme expressions. However, during a hiatus in proceedings the Presiding Officer, idly flicking through the manual, discovered that an expression of intention to desert was not admissible evidence, so almost all that the WAAF had written had to be crossed out. We, having drunk further mugs of tea, pinned to our several sheets of crossed out evidence the sole exhibit, a picture postcard of Cork harbour addressed to the station commander expressing the absentee's best wishes. The presiding officer then announced his need to relieve himself and that therefore the court would now rise.

We did have another case of desertion. In this case the offender was speedily caught and incarcerated in the guardroom. Thrice daily he had to be taken, handcuffed to a police corporal, to the airmen's mess for meals, which involved walking along a public road. The prisoner begged to be spared the humiliation of being seen in irons, so having given his word that he would not try to escape was unshackled. He immediately made off and outran the police corporal.

The sergeant in charge of the service police was a particularly unpleasant man (when eating in the Sergeants' Mess he kept his (loaded) revolver on the table beside his plate). Anyway, he was particularly beastly to the unfortunate corporal and when the escapee was recaptured he decreed that he personally would escort the prisoner to meals. Incredibly, the first time he did this he too was bamboozled into removing the handcuffs and again the man ran off and took refuge in the Polish WAAFs' compound. The police sergeant immediately summoned his squad and, accompanied by a Polish WAAF sergeant, searched this barbed-wire compound. The man was not found, nor was he ever heard of again. The police sergeant shortly afterwards was relieved of his duties!

We obviously followed the news of the war in the Pacific and how, as the Americans island-hopped westwards, the Japanese fought to the last, defending every indefensible bit of rock, each more fiercely than the last as the Americans approached Japan. I think most of us assumed that once all the islands had been cleaned up the new war could begin in earnest. I suppose we ought to have thought that having missed D-Day we would welcome the opportunity to make amends by taking part in the invasion of Japan. However, that is not how we saw it.

I have to admit that none of us appreciated the import of the newspaper headlines about a new American bomb. It was well known that during the war in Europe that size of bombs the American Flying Fortresses could carry was almost derisory when compared with those carried by our Lancasters, and some thought that this was merely news that with their new B29s the Yanks had caught up with us. There was news of a second bomb, and apparently exaggerated reports of 'widespread damage'.

When a few days later the end came with unexpected suddenness we really could not take it in that this was IT. All work stopped and there was a certain amount of unseemly rejoicing, culminating in an all-ranks party centred on the Sergeant's Mess, where there was the incautious consumption of alcohol of every kind followed by an impromptu singsong and dance that lasted until well after dawn. Judging by the number of couples who temporally absented themselves, some celebrations were of a more private nature.

The next morning those who could muster transport made for London, where there was in all honesty nothing much to do except be carried along in the walk-across-the-heads-of crowds that packed the West End, and gawp at people making fools of themselves. I myself saw a lady lieutenant colonel atop a lamppost outside Buckingham Palace greeting the royal balcony appearance with a song that I am sure the King would not have wished the princesses to hear. The abandoning of inhibitions was manifest in other ways, particularly in the parks. I remember seeing a lady hastily adjusting her attire whilst a trouserless lieutenant colonel, who had various bits of rubbish adhering to his tunic, was in acrimonious dispute with an RAF flight sergeant. It would seem that the flight sergeant had objected to the canine behaviour of the colonel and his lady and had, in the absence of a bucket of water, emptied a refuse basket over them.

Not all celebration was as unsavoury. I recall seeing a sailor, an airman and a couple of soldiers re-enacting a commando raid in St James' Park using a park bench as a landing craft. More august was the sight of the Athenaeum Club flambeaux in full fiery fury. (Gas-fuelled flaming cauldrons had been installed in pre-street-lamp times, to discourage cut-purses from molesting members; latterly lit only on great national celebrations such as Coronations or Jubilees.)

16

Coming Down to Earth

WE CARRIED ON training glider pilots, presumably because if we stopped no one knew what else they would find for us to do. In fact, what to do with aircrew generally must have been a poser for the authorities. Similarly, all aircrew training continued with newly-qualified aircrew piling up on a daily basis.

At the same time, most aircrew were young and owed their survival to being latecomers. A release system based on age and length of service meant that many young aircrew were insensitively called 'redundant' and were drafted into non-flying posts vacated by older and longer-serving people. It was a rather sad time. I recall officers being employed as tractor drivers and much-decorated senior NCOs being in junior clerical jobs.

We were fortunate, as what would now be called a job share was introduced, whereby we would be pilots for half a day and do something else for the other half. This was all right for some, but not for me. I was appointed officer in charge of Clothing Stores and my immediate task was to sign for the alleged contents of a vast building, stuffed to the rafters with every sort of garment, obtainable only through retail sources against clothing coupons. Shoes, socks, shirts, vests, pants, ties, uniforms and greatcoats were there in staggering abundance.

Hitherto an item offered for sale bearing the Crown-surmounted by an AM logo was obviously stolen. Now in these immediate post-war times, a great deal of equipment of every sort was being sold off, so 'Alexander MacCarthy's Crown Brand' no longer denoted dodginess. Thus theft thrived on an industrial scale.

Now obviously one should make a complete stock-take before signing for an inventory, but the outgoing inventory-holder invariably had to catch a train or whatever and one just had to give a quick glance and accept his assurance that it was all there. This was all a little daunting when that individual was about to become a civilian, as likely as not at some remote antipodean homestead.

One colleague had on his charge a hut containing many thousands of 'Beds, Folding, Airmen and Airwomen, For The Use Of'. (Presumably joint occupation was not envisaged.) All the windows of the hut were blacked out and, clearly as a result of an effort to stow every last bed, the doorway was jammed with an impenetrable mass of these beds. When he took over the inventory, checking was impossible, but they had been there for years and presumably would be there forever.

Then one day a lorry showed up with authorisation to collect something like 100 beds; it turned out that the forty or so beds jammed into the doorway were the sum total and the rest of the hut was one big empty space!

Such deficiencies, though serious at the time, could usually be amicably remedied by creative paperwork. One heard of 'replacements' for stolen Jeeps being conjured out of thin air for a few bottles of whisky. I even knew of a crew stealing a Lancaster bomber from another station to oblige a popular female equipment officer, who had found herself one short. In fact, one heard of aircraft shortages being remedied by creating fictitious accidents to enable the missing machine to be declared a write-off.

Whilst deficiencies might be remedied by creative accounting or theft, surpluses were another matter altogether since the unauthorised possession of equipment was a most serious offence. Small items could buried or burnt; larger ones could not, and became the cause of severe embarrassment. There was a persistent rumour that a surplus glider formed the basis for a profitable firewood business. One colleague in charge of Motor Transport found a more ready solution to the problem of over-stock. Discovering he had one too many motorcycles, he took the obvious course of painting one black and riding it home. My sole experience of 'unauthorised possession' was when I was (fortunately briefly) in charge of the Sergeants' Mess bar stock and found myself with a surplus of gin amounting to an appreciable number of cases. Happily, it was also found that the beer stock was deficient, hence the books could be squared by topping up part-used barrels with gin. It proved a mistake, since I was pressed to stay on since the beer in my care was said to have never been better kept.

Anyway, as far as this Clothing Stores was concerned, I was lumbered. I was assisted by 'helpful' NCOs who saw to all the paperwork, but oddly whenever a form was proffered for signature it was obscured by a big hairy hand leaving only the signature box exposed. If one asked to read the form there would be regretful tut-tutting that their help should be so scorned. 'Don't worry about a thing, sir. Just leave everything to us.'

All this lovely kit for which I found myself responsible was issued free to other ranks in exchange for old items that the Officer i/c Clothing Stores (me!) had certified as 1. Clean; 2. Unserviceable and beyond economic repair; 3. Free of evidence of improper use.

Only when I realised that the garments which had to be scrutinised to establish that they met these criteria included WAAF intimate apparel did I appreciate the weight of the responsibility that rested on my young shoulders. Actually, WAAF clothing exchanges were delegated to one of my WAAF staff, but in case of dispute they could still call on me to give a ruling as to whether a feminine undergarment should be replaced or merely required say, new elastic. Or, even worse, I had to decide if the garment's state of unserviceability was due to 'improper use'!

Items of uniform, besides offering less risk of embarrassment, were less marketable so possessed less entrepreneurial attraction. However, since officers wore the same battledress as airmen, moral dilemmas could arise. Airmen could exchange old for new but officers had to pay. Sometimes an officer would come in and put a well-worn battledress blouse and trousers on the counter, muttering something about dropping them in for exchange for one of his men who was too busy to bring them himself. The most cursory glance would reveal that officers' shoulder-braid had recently been removed. Also revealed would be a 10/- note which represented the market rate for 'failing to notice' the giveaway evidence.

Actually, officer purchases were a nuisance, as without them the stores just handed out new garments in exchange for old so the total of old and new clothes added up to the correct number. However, introducing money into the equation complicated matters, producing a powerful incentive to follow the unofficial route instanced above.

Of course, if the total of, say, 'Trousers, Blue-Grey, Airmen For The Use Of' failed to tally, 'steps' had to be 'taken'. Since the number of garments, but not their condition seemed to matter, additional 'pairs' of trousers could be 'created' by tearing old ones in half. Indeed, the competence of a storekeeper might be judged by his ability to trisect a shirt.

I eventually found an officer in great distress, as he just could not cope with being responsible for a zillion pounds worth of Link Trainers, as the primitive flight simulators of the day were called. On the premise that these gadgets were of no domestic value, were too big to be smuggled out and, anyway, were bolted to the floor, I was happy to swap my Clothing Store for his Link Trainer section. So delighted was he with the transaction that, as I recall, he insisted that I accepted a small sum for my trouble.

Most people had a 'sideline'. One sergeant dealt in jewellery and would rent out brass 'wedding rings' to enable young ladies to be passed off as wives when seeking hotel accommodation. With prices escalating, car dealing was an obvious source of profit. One chap combined the two – he took a diamond ring exchange for a Railton car.

One flight commander, having been out shooting rabbits before breakfast, spent the morning skinning, cleaning and then delivering them to nearby restaurants.

Another less profitable way of pretending to be busy was the EVT scheme. This was a grand plan of Educational and Vocational Training, a well-intentioned and not altogether unsuccessful attempt to make service personnel fit to become ex-service personnel. EVT also provided an opportunity to spread ourselves a little more thinly so maintaining the need for pilots despite a diminishing task load.

You could either be an instructor, a student or, as in my case, both. The core of instructors were academics and others whose particular, and often great, expertise found little demand in the military market, so had spent the war in various unskilled roles. Now promoted to sergeant they often cut somewhat un-NCO-like figures. One course I opted for was Business Studies, the instructor having been a Petticoat Lane trader with a sharp nose for a profit. However, his concept of double entry bookkeeping seemed to be one entry for yourself and the other entry for the taxman. Lectures were delivered in Cockney rhyming slang and were largely unintelligible. Another course was typing, taught by a well-known lady novelist of the bodice-ripper genre, who insisted I join her on the floor. I assumed she wanted to develop some ideas for her next steamy opus, but she only wanted me to balance a Remington portable on my stomach and touch-type 'The quick brown fox' etc. I don't think I ever acquired even a modicum of keyboard skills.

On the other side of the desk, as it were, I was, on the strength of several weeks' self-taught experience and ownership of a Rudge Ulster, no less, to become an official motorcycling instructor, a position entitling me to a special issue of petrol coupons. The driving instructor fared even better; he had the use of a van and having convinced the Orderly Room that traffic experience was essential, regularly went to Birmingham and beyond.

With everything winding down and a surplus of people, EVT was pushed to the limit to keep people occupied – almost anything could be studied; anyone proclaiming the most arcane career intentions, would be liable to have an instructor found and a course created. It was said that should an airman and an airwoman be discovered in flagrante, as it were, they would only have to claim that they were doing their homework for the EVT biology course.

Apart from EVT and job-sharing there was, when summer came round again, the opportunity to do farm work. If done at weekends one earned an enhanced rate of a little over 3/- (15p). Oddly, although this represented the best part of a day's pay to an airman, only more senior men took it up.

I was employed by Air Commodore R. H. Verney, DL, CBE, RAF (Ret.), a delightful chap who, after serving as a Royal Flying Corps pilot, entered the RAF Technical Procurement Department. He was largely responsible for British participation in the Schneider Trophy Air Races, which led to the development of the Spitfire. Having reached air rank comparatively young, his career stalled when he ordered fifty aircraft of a totally unproven type which lacked any form of defensive armament and were made of plywood! This ridiculous machine was the war-winning Mosquito! This could be flown by two men, against the ten needed to man a B17 'Flying Fortress', the mainstay of the US army air corps, whose bomb load was scarcely more than the Mosquito and was much more vulnerable to enemy attack.

A member of an aristocratic family, Verney farmed with his brother, who had been an engineer commander in the Navy. Despite the loss of an arm he had a magnificent workshop with machine tools driven by steam engines that he had designed

163

and built himself. He had just finished wiring the estate houses for electricity, and manufactured some otherwise unobtainable parts for my motorcycle, adhering to his maxim: 'If a component fails, establish why it has failed and replace it with a suitably improved part.'

The Verney brothers were looked after by their sister, a statuesque lady whose long blonde hair half concealed the parrot that lived on her shoulder, its droppings encrusting her Paisley shawl. She made delightful cakes, which she insisted I ate in vast quantities.

By this time, Croughton had closed and our whole outfit was moved to the coupled stations of Wellesbourne Mountford and Gaydon. We seemed to alternate between the two, Wellesbourne being the preferred address. Firstly, one had one's own room with a young German prisoner-of-war servant, whereas at Gaydon we had to fend for ourselves, six to a hut. Secondly, Wellesbourne offered opportunity for profit. It had accommodated a Photographic Unit, which had left us with a suite of darkrooms with sinks, safe lights, dishes and a print dryer. Someone got hold of an enlarger, a supply of film and paper appeared and between us we had several cameras. For a modest fee we would do portraits, people posing alongside their cars or on their motorcycles and of aircrew alongside their aircraft. For a somewhat enhanced fee we would do plane-to-plane pictures, in sizes up to full plate. By experiment we found we could extrapolate the time/temperature tables for developing and fixing to near boiling point. I recall that provided the picture was taken alongside the photographic section, we could produce a print within three or four minutes. Since the section was close to the gate, we could stop passers-by, especially those with dogs or children, and do a while-you-wait 'photographic study'.

In due course, my number came up and I joined the unseemly rush for the exit. In my case, that was Wembley Stadium, where one was issued with a piece of paper that in every case certified that one's competence was 'average' and one's conduct had been 'satisfactory'. I was, of course, provided with a set of civilian clothes, which in my case were described as being for the 'short and portly'.

Having obtained, by some devious means which I forget, the necessary clothing coupons, I had recently treated myself to a tailor-made suit, so was able to pass up the offer of a 'de-mob suit' and took a sports jacket and trousers instead. One could not quite read a newspaper through the trousers but the jacket served me well, and I discarded it only when I became 'short and portlier'. The shirt was passable, as was the tie, the shoes were fair – but the pullover was a gem. I still find it useful for gardening on chilly days.

So with release papers, eight weeks' pay, ration book and a pound of tobacco, I presented my Railway Warrant at Paddington station.

17

Coda

HITLER, HIROHITO AND the rest of the evil gang murdered millions and caused countless millions more to perish as the consequence of conflict, yet they unwittingly enabled me not only to learn to fly but to do so from the best instructors of the best Air Force in the world. Moreover, refugees from Hitler ensured that the genie was let out of the bottle at Los Alamos in time to enable me to survive to fly for sixty years after King George and I went our separate ways – indeed, also to outlive the Wolverhampton trolleybuses that were the catalyst of my flying career. What sort of 'survivor's guilt' does that engender?

After an interval of almost a decade and a half I had the opportunity, thanks to having Tubby Wild's name in my log-book, to re-join the RAF on a part-time basis, the formalities of doing so being sealed by a letter from Her Most Gracious Majesty addressing me as her 'Trusty and Well Beloved', which was rather nice of her considering that the only time our paths had crossed was on VJ-day when she waved to me from the balcony of Buckingham Palace.

I found that some things had changed: no one called people of equal or near-equal rank by their surnames; 'sir' had largely been replaced by 'boss', and the term 'pilot officer' now extended to little girls. (Even in the swinging sixties, the idea of a female in the crew room, let alone in the cockpit, could cause apoplexy.) The food was better and the flight mechanics, now all of the male persuasion, wore the sort of bad weather clothing our girls would have given their little all for in the old days.

Remembering the times when chicken was a rare delicacy confined to the officers' mess, and then only when entertaining honoured guests, to hear mutinous mumblings from airmen about too much chicken was an eye-opener. As was hearing an officer refusing to fly because he had to wash his car.

By far the biggest shock was seeing that the parade ground, once the sacred territory of robotic Station Warrant Officers on which no man or woman dared set foot, was now a car park. Concomitant with that, every inch of the Air Force's sovereign territory was a bicycle-free zone. Everyone had a motor vehicle, although in the usual topsy-turvy way of things, a senior officer's transport could well be a moped; any Jaguar around the place would probably belong to a corporal.

Many things were unchanged, especially the high standard of skills, both in the air and in the hangers – in fact, they were even higher. Even so, there were still some officers apparently commissioned by clerical error. I had one flight commander who stuffed all correspondence that he did not understand (which was most of it) down behind the filing cabinets. His flying ability was so lacking that a master pilot had to be posted in to conduct our periodic flying tests (the master pilot was a senior non-commissioned pilot, of which there were still a few survivors from the time when pilots were not necessarily officers). This Flt Commander could cause a great deal of hilarity, such as when in a crowded crew room, I told him he was a ***** idiot; he went very red and putting his face close to mine saying: 'I bet you are not man enough to repeat that in private'.

Fortunately such incompetence was rare, but there were plenty of oddballs such as another flight commander who, every three months, made and deep-froze enough sandwiches to make himself thirteen weeks-worth of packed lunches. There was another who came back from leave with innumerable 'holiday snaps' to show to anyone who failed to evade him. On one occasion he returned, not from holiday, but from a spell in hospital following a riding accident. He had no photographs, so we were forced to look at a sheaf of X-ray plates.

There was the diminutive elderly squadron leader who used to recount how, as an AC2 (Aircraftman second class) he was an amateur jockey, whose talent for 'pulling' a horse could ensure that the 'right' one won. Apparently at some far-flung outstation this remarkable and potentially profitable ability was noticed on high, with the result that he was commissioned so he could be housed in the officer's mess, where he could be kept safe from investors who required a different result. It seems that prior to a big race when large sums were dependent on his skills, he was posted to a far distant unit. Fortuitously a vacancy for a senior officer arose, so his services were retained by promoting him to squadron leader to fill it.

Probably the oddest was an army officer with whom I found myself sharing a room. He slept naked on top of the bedclothes and breakfasted on Brown Ale, plenty of which was available from the numerous crates of it that cluttered the room.

I was glad to find that my knack of inadvertently annoying my betters remained undiminished. After all, how was I to know in a small mess that the crossword in the only copy of the *Daily Telegraph* was by common consent reserved for the PMC (President of the Messing Committee)? How was I supposed to know that the cretin on the other end of the telephone was a brigadier? Nor this time was it my fault that, a quarter of a century on, I blocked 617 Squadron's runway.

Also, it seems, the public perception of the RAF was altered. Picture myself and an equally middle-aged officer seated in one of the old and much missed six-seater railway compartments. A couple of giggling girls appear at the corridor window and somewhat to our annoyance, start to slide open the corridor door. Then one says to the other: 'We'd better not go in this one, they're raff boys and you know what they are like!'

Happily still proving as immutable as the Laws of the Medes

and the Persians, was The System and all its paradoxes, as was demonstrated when four of us, having delivered four two-seater aircraft, needed transport to where we had left our cars at another airfield some 50 miles away. A suitable aeroplane not being available, a minibus, driver and an officer with enough clout to authorise the journey were found.

Unfortunately, there was insufficient diesel in the minibus for the round trip. Being after 5 pm the guy in charge of the diesel pump had gone home and no officer sufficiently senior to authorise the purchase of fuel from civilian sources could be found. Since the driver assured us that one gallon would suffice we decided that we would pick up fuel on the way, for which we would gladly pay.

The idea was greeted with shock and horror. Apparently the Air Force grasped that persons might want to steal motor fuel and a system of checks and balances, backed up by severe penalties, was in place to thwart this. However, the idea that anyone should actually wish to donate motor fuel was totally outside the comprehension envelope: at best we must be Soviet spies; visions of incarceration in the Tower loomed. As I recall we reached our cars by returning in two of the aircraft, leaving the matter of their re-delivery as someone else's problem.

Then there was the matter of life jackets. An order came out stating that dire penalties awaited anyone flying within a certain distance from the coast without such a garment. At the end of the promulgation was an addendum: 'This order does not apply if the relevant equipment is unavailable.'

On one occasion, at a bomber station during the height of the Cold War, my radio headset needed attention, but the only competent technician happened to be in a very secret, barbed-wire enclosed, Service-Police-sentinelled bunker. Even to a fully commissioned officer, with up-to-date security clearance, this was a 'need to know' area and there was nothing I needed to know within its curtilage.

Eventually a senior officer with sufficient clout to get me past the gate guardians was found. He was able to close-escort me to the appropriate department. When my escort and I eventually negotiated the labyrinthine corridors and came face to face with the appropriate technician, he turned out to be Chinese.

When I first joined up I gained the impression that corporals ran the Air Force and that officers existed purely for ornamental and ceremonial purposes. I soon learned that this was not strictly true, but the fact that the technician in the secret bunker was a corporal revived the old suspicion that mystical powers could accompany two stripes. One could not help thinking of the legend of the King's Corporal, a rank allegedly personally conferred by the Sovereign on soldiers who in pre-medal days had performed some notable service to said sovereign. There was also the preposterous notion that somewhere in Whitehall's remotest recesses lurked a Delphic oracle-like corporal who was consulted by the chiefs of staff on all matters of import.

The possibility that there was some iota of truth in these legends was made manifest to me some years after Her Majesty and I went our separate ways.

An RAF MU (Maintenance Unit) had invited me to tender for some German technical equipment. I did my sums and submitted a tender good for thirty days. A week or two after the tender had expired, I received an order. Since the Mark had risen sharply, I had to point out that the tender had expired and I could only accept the order at an increase of 15 per cent due to the now less favourable exchange rate.

The upshot was, I was invited to attend the MU to 'discuss' the matter. Once there, a flight lieutenant suggested that the Officer's Mess bar might be more comfortable than his office to 'sort the matter out'. There, over a drink, it became apparent that his idea of sorting the matter out meant accepting the original figure. When I refused he pointed out that unless they had the gear pronto, the country would be defenceless against the Communist hordes, and if we found ourselves overrun by Russians in a nuclear desert, it would be all my fault. Next, a squadron leader appeared and went through the same gambit, putting in a few 'Sirs'. When that failed, a wing commander was sent for. He insisted I have a double single malt and addressed me as 'Old Boy' while admitting that he might be able to persuade Group to accept 10 per cent. When I said 'No way, José', he petulantly complained that he would have to go 'right to the top' and stamped off in a huff.

A few days later a cultured and authoritative voice on the telephone announced, 'MOD here. Regarding our order no xxx, I understand that you wish to increase your price. Some currency problem, I believe.'

Before I could say anything, he went on, 'That's not a problem – can you go ahead on my say-so? I'll confirm it by fax, of course'.

Imagining a cuff with so much braid that it was an effort to lift the phone, I stood to attention before answering: 'Yes, sir, certainly sir'.

'Well done', he said as if pinning a medal on one. 'We're cutting a few corners here so you may run into a few snags. If so, do use my name'.

'Sorry sir, but I didn't quite catch your name, sir', I managed to stammer.

He told me, I noted it.

'What is your rank, sir?' I said trying to remember if there were two Ls in Marshal.

'Corporal', came the reply.

Books by
Alun John Richards

A Gazeteer of the Welsh Slate Industry

Gazateer of Slate Quarrying in Wales

Slate Quarrying at Corris

Slate Quarrying in Wales

Slate Quarrying in Pembrokeshire

The Slate Regions of North and Mid-Wales

Fragments of Mine & Mill

The Slate Railways of Wales

Welsh Slate Craft

Crefft Llechi

Tinplate in Wales

Rails & Sails of Welsh Slate

A Swansea Boy

Cwm Gwyrfai
(with Gwynfor Pierce Jones)

A Tale of Two Rivers
(with Jean Napier)

Two Snowdonia Rivers
(with Jean Napier)

Conway Source to Sea
(with Jean Napier)